Charles H. Simpson

Life in the Far West

Adventures Among the Indians and Outlaws of Montana

Charles H. Simpson

Life in the Far West
Adventures Among the Indians and Outlaws of Montana

ISBN/EAN: 9783743367395

Manufactured in Europe, USA, Canada, Australia, Japa

Cover: Foto ©ninafisch / pixelio.de

Manufactured and distributed by brebook publishing software (www.brebook.com)

Charles H. Simpson

Life in the Far West

LIFE IN THE FAR WEST,

— OR —

A DETECTIVE'S

THRILLING ADVENTURES

— AMONG —

THE INDIANS AND OUTLAWS

OF MONTANA.

———:o:———

— BY

C. H. SIMPSON.

———:o:———

CHICAGO

RHODES & McCLURE PUBLISHING COMPANY.

1897.

-:CONTENTS:-

————:o:————

"OH, BUT WON'T I HAVE A TIME."

WILD LIFE IN FAR WEST,

—: OR :—

A DETECTIVE'S THRILLING ADVENTURES

AMONG

THE INDIANS AND OUTLAWS OF MONTANA.

CHAPTER I.

AN IMPORTANT DECISION.

''The tenth of March!'' cried Charley Shipton, a young detective, who had just been notified that he was to have a summer's vacation beginning upon the tenth of March. Glad news was this for the young fellow; for he had been working hard and faithfully for the last two years and deserved, if any one did, a recognition of his faithful services.

Happy and light hearted was Charley Shipton when the welcome and long looked for tidings were received.

''The tenth of March'' he mused, ''let me see; just five days—O but wont I have a time! and dancing a hornpipe in his glee, he shouted:

''Bully for us!''

''Hello!'' cried Fred Wilson, an old chum of Charley's entering the room at this opportune moment—just in

(9)

time to hear Charley's exuberant though somewhat vulgar expression, where he stood aghast and bewildered at the queer antics of his usually sober and altogether businesslike room-mate.

"Bully!" again cried the overjoyed fellow, shaking the welcome missive before the eyes of his "pard," as he called his chum. "Bully for me!" kawhoop. I'm off!"

"By thunder Charley, I believe you are off!" exclaimed Fred. "What the deuce have you been imbibing anyhow old fellow: Rock and rye, or plain bugjuice?"

"Nary one," shouted Charley. "It's better than that. No, no Fred, no Rock and rye, no spiderjuice, but a straight out and out summer's vacation."

"P-h-e-u," whistled Fred". By gum though, Charley I envy your good luck, though you deserve it all right enough. But where are you going—to see your folks out in Kansas?"

"No. I may go there, but not to stay. I am off on a regular old tare. Don't know yet just where I will go; but I think I will go to the mountains."

"Let's see" said his friend, here is a map of the United States, let's look." And spreading it out upon the table, the two friends sat down and began to look up a desirable locality; a place where a lover of adventuresome sport would be most likely to find what his heart had for so many years craved, a place where hunting and fishing and possibly something of a more adventuresome character, as well, could be found.

Looking over the broad domain of the United States and for a moment with finger poised in a debating attitude, it descended and rested upon a spot near the Yellowstone Park in the far away territory of Wyoming.

"Yes, Fred, I will go there. It's the wildest part of the United States," he said and that's just what I want. I want to get away from civilization, from the rush and roar of the city from fashion and from—from—

"The fair sex" suggested Fred, with a shrug of his broad shoulders.

"Yes. I will have summer all by myself at anyrate," said Charley; "and that will be a relief.

"Bet you will be homesick before you've been gone a month."

"Well, homesick, lovesick or what-sick, I am off," replied Charley.

And five days later he took the train for Miles City, the then western terminus of the Northern Pacific Railroad, where he arrived in due course of time.

Here, he learned, that a day's drive from Terry Station, some fifty miles below, that that noble game, the American buffalo, were to be found in great plenty.

This was a temptation altogether too great for the sport loving detective; so he decided to turn from his course just long enough to take a day or two among the shaggy monsters.

The route was down the Yellowstone River; and the quickest and easiest mode of conveyance was by boat. So a boat was procured and all articles necessary for a three or four days grand buffalo hunt were loaded into the boat, and soon he found himself, in company with a young fellow, whom he had picked up, upon the swift, turbulant current of the Yellowstone.

Down the swift, rushing river they glided, rivaling the speed of a race-horse in their mad career. Pleasant, indeed, was the journey. Beautiful scenery lined the river's course upon either hand. Now upon the one side, high bluffs, barren and broken, with dark canons and narrow, winding defiles which looked as if they might have been the retreat of banditti or bold, daring highwaymen; then upon the other side, the country stretching away as far as the eye could reach in broad, undulating plains, with here and there, nestling beside some little stream and sheltered by the spreading branches of giant cottonwoods, was to be seen the homes of the much talked of "Cow-boy," while over the grassy plains roamed their herds of horses and cattle.

On, on they flew; till, presently, they heard a dull, roaring sound, which came to them from down the river, like the distant roar of a cataract.

"What is it?" asked Charley of his companion.

"It's Buffalo Rapids," replied he. "We'd better pull in near the shore, for we'll have to land. We can't run the rapids in such a small boat."

But it was too late, for already the swift current was drawing them on with that irresistable force and speed which convinced them that escape was impossible.

Swiftly they were approaching now; while Charley, standing in the bow of the boat, paddle in hand, his eagle-eye scanning the foaming, leaping water, on it poured over the line of ugly rocks which stretched from shore to shore, watched for a passage through which to pass.

On, on, now upon the verge of the rapids, the black, ugly rocks thrusting their jagged heads above the water upon either side; then, with a plunge like a frightened bird descending from on high, the little boat shot down through the hissing, roaring current. There was a plunge, a roar, and, in an instant, the little boat shot triumphantly out from the torrent of foam and spray and rested upon the placid waters below.

"By jingoes," exclaimed Charley, "I would like to do it again!"

"Excuse me," declared his companion, "I don't want any more of that in mine!"

Not long after, they reached the landing at Terry Station where they landed and were joined by a man with teams whom Charley had hired to go with him upon the hunt.

The next morning, bright and early, the teams were hitched up and they pulled out for the buffalo range, some thirty miles to the southward.

Along toward evening, having reached a favorable locality, they went into camp upon the bank of a little stream and prepared for a grand hunt upon the morrow.

————:o:————

CHAPTER II.

Early the next morning Charley shouldered his Winchester rifle and started out for his first Buffalo hunt. Climbing the high bluffs which lead to the broad table-lands above, stretching away as far as the eye could reach, he beheld a sight that made his heart bound with a feeling of joy and gratification; for, scarcely two miles away, he discovered a small herd of buffaloes quietly grazing upon the grassy plain.

Walking a short distance around to the lee side—for he knew that the buffalo was a keen scented animal—he worked his way up to within a hundred yards or so, and singling out the finest specimen, sent a bullet just back of his huge, shaggy shoulders. With an inexpress-ible feeling of joy he saw that the great brute was mor-tally wounded. Again, and again, he discharged his gun, but, seemingly, with no further effect than to hasten their precipitate retreat. But the first shot was entirely satisfactory, and, I must confess, very credible as well; for he had killed his first buffalo, and that. too, with his first shot.

As the great, shaggy fellow, who had run for a few rods, went down, Charley ran up to him and standing beside the fallen monster, waved his hat and, with an air of triumph, shouted—

"Ka-whoop—bully for us!"

Just then the report of fire-arms away off to the south came to him and a little later, the bold hnnter was over-joyed at seeing a small herd of buffalo making

My First Buffalo.

slowly over the bluffs in a direction that would lead them not far from where he stood.

It was but the work of a few minutes for the swift-footed hunter to gain a position directly in their path, where, concealing himself behind a large rock, he awaited their approach.

Five minutes passed, then the shaggy humps of the king of American game appeared above the ridge, and a moment later they stood in full view.

Oh what a sight to make glad the heart of the hunter! Scarcely twenty yards away stood the noble game. All unconcious of the near presence of his deadly foe, stood a lordly bull—a very giant among his fellows.

"Ah!" muttered the hunter, his eyes sparkling, his heart bounding, as he glanced along the deadly, shining barrel of his gun for one brief moment. Bang! rang out the death knell, and, as the red fire leaped from the muzzle of his rifle, the shaggy lord of the plains went down.

Again the note of death rang out and another went down; but almost at the same instant came a report from the opposite side of the herd and a bullet passed through the crown of his hat so close that it clipped a lock of hair from his head.

"By ginger," muttered Charley, "that fellow missed his mark but came mighty near catching me!" But nothing daunted he raised his gun again and fired. Another buffalo went down, and again came the sharp crack of a rifle from the other side of the herd, which, undecided which way to go, had remained nearly stationary while the shooting was going on.

"Oh, arn't this glorious!" muttered the fortunate

hunter; and he raised his gun for a fourth shot, when again rang out that sharp crack from over the other side; and this time the bullet struck the rock directly in front of his face, filling his eyes with dirt and, for a moment, completely blinding him.

"By thunder," exclaimed Charley, "that shot was intended for me! Ah, my fine fellow, I can show you a trick worth a half dozen of that. And slipping back a few paces, and down the hill so that he would be out of sight, he walked rapidly around the hill in a direction that soon brought him upon the same side, and behind the point from whence the shots had been fired that came so near ending his life. But nothing of his unseen enemy could be seen.

"Ah, he must have been up there among those rocks," mused the young hunter; "that's just the position he would choose and it is just the point from whence that shot came. By ginger now, I will know about that if he is there!" and crawling silently up to the place, he peered about among the rocks but failed to find the object of his search. But, after a close examination, he discovered where the man had been crouching behind a rock. "Ah," he said, "he must be a good shot, for I was over a hundred yards away and he couldn't see me, only when I would raise up to fire. By thunder," he exclaimed, examining the tracks, "that was an Indian so help me bob!"

A little further examination showed that the Indian had adopted the same tactics to surprise him that he had to surprise the Indian, for the Indian had gone around the hill in the same direction which Charley had taken, and arrived upon the opposite side at about the same time.

"By ginger now, but this is getting interesting," declared Charley. No doubt, the Indian was thinking the same from his side of the hill, and, like Charley, wondering what to do next.

Here again, as before, both were of the same notion; for Charley determined to settle the matter at all hazards, and, going around the hill in the same direction taken by the Indian, he soon came to a point upon the same side and not more than a twenty or thirty yards from where he was concealed when the Indian had shot at him.

"By ginger!" he exclaimed, as he saw how completely he would have been at the mercy of his foe had he remained in his former position till the Indian had reached the spot. "Phew, but wouldn't he have ripped me up the back though if I had stayed here! Ugh!" he shuddered," I believe I will go back to camp. And suiting the action to the word, he turned down the ravine, in the head of which he was standing, and started for camp.

————:o:————

CHAPTER III.

Walking rapidly down the ravine, Charley, in the course of half an hour, came out upon a high hill overlooking the valley in which his camp was situated.

Before reaching the summit of the ridge from whence his camp could be seen, he had noticed a column of white smoke rising above the hill-top and in the direction of the camp which caused him to quicken his pace. Hurrying on and wondering what was the meaning of it, he saw, as he stood upon the hill, a sight which caused him to pause with a feeling of horror at his heart that would be hard to describe. Before him, stretched out the broad valley of O'Fallan creek, and not a half mile away, where he had left his little camp, was now but a smouldering pile of embers.

"By thunder," cried Charley excitedly, "I wonder if those Indians have surprised the boys and killed them and then plundered and burned the camp? I can't see anything of the boys nor the Indians, but there's the horses; they havn't meddled with them—ah, by gum, now, I wonder if they are lying in ambush awaiting my return." But not a trace of anyone could be seen. "What does it mean?" he wondered; "what the deuce is to pay anyway? By ginger, now, but I will solve this riddle, so help me bob!"

As we have already stated, Charley Shipton was not only brave, but daring, and, at times, even approaching recklessness. At that time and under the then existing circumstances, it was indeed not much short of reckless-

(18)

A "RED DEVIL."

ness that prompted him to the bold move that he made; for quickly descending the high bluff, he strode boldly across the valley to the camp.

But there were no Indians waiting in ambush there. Had there been, this story would not have been written, and this "Summer Vacation" would have come to an untimely end.

Not a trace of the Indians was to be seen; nor could he tell to any certainty whether the camp had been plundered or not, as everything was burned.

"By ginger," muttered Charley, -'I can't make this out! Why the dickens didn't they take the horses too? But perhaps they couldn't catch them—lucky for us anyway. But where's the boys? what—ah, here they come!" he exclaimed, as his two companions appeared, coming from down the valley.

Neither of them had seen anything of the Indians, but a careful examination showed them the moccasin tracks of a half dozen or so of them.

"Oh, but I would like to make them pay for this, though," declared Charley.

"We'd better get out of this before they return and take our scalps," suggested the others, evincing no little alarm.

Much as Charley would like to have had another day's hunt, he could not persuade the others to stay any longer; so they brought up the horses and went some ten miles west where they went into camp for the night.

As it wanted a couple of hours yet till sun-set, Charley took his gun and went out in the hope of finding another buffalo, but in this he was disappointed; so taking down a deep canon, he started to return to camp.

Following the canon for some two miles, he turned a bend in the canon and came suddenly upon an Indian encampment. There were a dozen or more wigwams and a score of painted savages.

Just as he came in sight, an Indian rode into camp from down the canon, and by his excited manner it was plainly evident that he had discovered the hunter's camp, which was only about two miles below.

''By thunder," exclaimed Charley, ''those are the same fellows that burnt my camp! Look at that red devil, he's got.my Sunday coat on, and my boots.—Oh, you dirty devil, how I would like to send a bullet through your hide! They've discovered our camp, I know from that fellows actions—I wonder what they will do anyway? They look ugly enough to do anything. By ginger now, if they were to take into their heads to attack us, they'd have our scalps dangliug on their lodge poles before morning. Ugh," he shuddered, ''I ain't quite ready yet. I want to live long enough to finish out my summer's vacation. By gum now, I've dreamed of all this, and thought how romantic and grand it would be to beard the 'noble red man' in his native wilds; but, durn my skin, if those devils don't look ugly!" And he began to cast about for a way to make his escape unseen, without going back the way he came.

''Yes," he mused, ''I believe I can creep up through that little gully yonder and cross the ridge without being seen, unless some of them happen to come this way. 'Spect I'd better do it." And shaking his fist at the Indians he stole silently away and was soon making his way up through the water-worn gully. Nearly half way up he was arrested by hearing approaching footsteps from above. It was so dark in the deep gully, that one could see but a few yards, but as the person was above him, his dark form was outlined against the sky, which showed plainly to the hunter that the approaching form was that of an Indian, returning to camp.

"By ginger," muttered Charley, "I am in for it now, whether I want to or not! D—d if I will go back—can't get out on either side—ain't room for us to pass by each other, and I won't lie down for him to pass over me, nor will he, for me to pass over him. By gum!" muttered Charley.

"Ugh!" grunted the Indian, and a moment more, the two men were locked in a deadly embrace.

Charley Shipton was a powerful, athletic man, fully six feet in height, nimble and wiry as a cat; but in spite of his Herculean strength and athletic training, he was met in every move and foiled in every attempt, by the wily savage.

Not a word was uttered by either; but now the heavy, labored breathing told but too plainly of the awful strain upon those sinews of steel.

"Ugh!" grunted the savage at last, reaching for his knife. This act gave Charley the long looked for advantage, and with one mighty effort he hurled the savage head-long down the steep gully. Bounding from rock to rock, then whirling through the air. he fell with a dull, sickening thud upon the jagged rocks below.

"Cratch-at-hemlock!" panted the triumphant hunter, as that sickening sound came up from below; and, with

a shudder, he turned and continued up the gully. Pausing for a moment, as he emerged upon the bluff, to
satisfy himself that no one was 'following him, he
resumed his retreat and soon after reached camp.

"What do you think, boys," he asked after telling his
adventure, "do you think that they will meddle
with us?"

"Bet your life they'll meddle with us, if they find out
that we are here, and especially if you killed that
fellow!"

"Killed him! I'll bet there wasn't a whole bone left in
his body. But they won't know it—they'll think he
fell. If he is killed, it's all right, but if he's alive, the
devil will be to pay."

D—n their hides," exclaimed one, "I know what's
up; they'll wait till night and then make an attack upon
us, run off our stock and, perhaps, put a bullet through
our skins, just to be a doing."

"By gum," cried Charley, "I don't like to be ruu off
like this!"

"We'd better git," declared the other two, so nothiug
was left but to go, which they immediately did, arriving
the next morning at the station.

That evening, while sitting in a billiard hall, Charley's
curiosity was aroused by the queer actions of an old
man who had entered at about the same time that
he had.

The keen, practical eye of the young detective told
him at a glance that the old man was working some
scheme—was, in all probability, a detective, and was
shadowing some one.

"By jinks!" mused Charley, "I will see, just for fun, what the old fellow is up to." And a very fortunate thing for the old man, too, it proved to be, as the developments of a few hours later showed.

————:o:————

CAAPTER IV.

A HARD CASE.

At about ten o'clock the old man arose to go, and, as he went out, a man who had been sitting reading a newspaper, carelessly threw his paper down, arose and left also. There was nothing peculiar about this, but somehow, Charley noticed the act, and could but think that the old man leaving had sometning to do with it.

"At any rate," mused Charley, as he followed the man out, "I'll see what he's up to." And following the man for a short distance, he became aware that he (the man whom he was following) was also following some one else—that one, he believed, was the old man.

Just out from the station a little ways was a large house, and to this house the old man went. The house was situated among a grove of large trees which partially hid it from view and, at the same time. offered a shelter to the old man who had worked his way around to the rear of the house and was scanning it closely.

At this stage of the game, the object of the man whom Charley was following, was plainly shown; for, with the the stealthiness of a cat the man crawled upon his victim, and in a moment, had grappled with him.

Struggling desperately, the old man endeavored to free himself from his assailant, but without avail. Taken at a great disadvantage, besides being the weaker of the two, the old man would soou have been disposed of, had not a timely aud unlooked for interference arrested the hand of the would-be assassin.

Locked in each others embrace they staggered and fei!. The old man was quickly at the mercy of his opponent,

A Detective Caught.

who, grappling his throat with his left hand, drew an ugly looking knife and, raising it aloof, he hissed—

"Curse you! you have reached the end of this trail, just as many smarter men than you have done before. You have undertaken a hard case—too hard for you!"

As he uttered these words, he aimed a blow full at the old man's breast. But the knife never descended — the hand was grasped in the vise-like grip of Charley's strong hand, while with one mighty effort he hurled the man to the ground and then, turning to the old man. he asked—

"Are you hurt?"

"No." he replied, rising to his feet.

"Well, you would have been presently, I think, from the way that he was operating."

"Do you know who he was?" asked the old man.

"No," replied Charley, "I don't know him."

"Do you live here?"

"No," replied Charley, "I am just stopping here for a little. But come down to camp with me, my friend. I would like to talk a little with you. You are a detective, I think—so am I, and I am off on a vacation—"

"Ah!" interrupted the old man, "and to that fact, I presume, I owe my life. Well, it was lucky for me at any rate."

"Yes," said Charley, he had you foul; but come, let's be off before he returns with help."

And, together, they went down to Charley's camp.

"I will tell you about this business," said the old man. "I have been working this case for a little over

a year.   But to begin at the beginning.   Two years ago
James Barnes, a wealthy merchant of New York, failing
in business, sought to retrieve his lost fortune by forgery.
Checks to the amount of several thousand dollars were
forged and for a long time, so skillful was the work
done, that it escaped detection.   Barnes himself did not
do the work, but he handled the forged checks.   The
work was done by his daughter, a girl of some fifteen
years of age.   The case was brought to us two years
ago, and work was begun immediately; and so persistent
and so hard did they press him, that he and his daughter
disappeared.   Since I took the case by myself, I have
traced him to this country.   But I have lost the trail
here.   But I've struck another.   There are two families
of these Barnes'.   The other family broke up in Cincinnati at about the same time that this one did.   He came
here too, and is now engaged in counterfeiting.   He has
two sons, who have been engaged in the business for
several years.   So, you see, it is a hard case.

"But this first Barnes, do you think that he is connected with the other in this business?" asked Charley.

"No doubt of it."

"And you have lost track of him, you say?"

"Yes."

"Do you think that there's anything here?"

"No, I am pretty certain that they are at Miles City
now."

"Then you will go up there, I suppose?" asked
Charley.

"Yes, and I would like to have you go with me, too,"
he replied.

"All right, I will go.   I am going west, and as long as the trail leads that way, I don't mind trying them a little."

"There's a reward of ten thousand dollars offered for the girl and her father.   Perhaps that this case here will throw some light on the other."

So it was decided, and a half hour later they took the train for Miles City.

On entering the passenger coach, Charley walked down the aisle, looking for a seat, as the coach was full. At last he found a seat with but one occupant—a beautiful girl of some fifteen or sixteen years of age.

"Do you object?" laughed Charley, as he sat down beside her.

"Don't think it would do any good if I did," she laughed; and her large, blue eyes sparkled mischievously as she met Charley's admiring glance.

Chatting pleasantly, the time passed quickly and almost before they were aware of it, Miles City was announced.

—————:O:—————

CHAAPTER V.

TRAPPED.

"Do you stop here?" asked Charley of his companion as the train stopped at the station.

"Yes," replied the girl. "do you?"

"Yes," he answered, "have you some one with you, or—"

"Yes, yes," interrupted the girl, casting a sly glance into his face; and then said quickly: "perhaps we may meet again—good bye."

"By ginger," mused Charley, "but she's a beauty and a regular little minx too. By jingoes now, I almost wish I was agoing to stay here awhile — I would like to get acquainted with her."

Little did he dream how soon he would get acquainted with her and the part that she was destined to play in his 'summer's vacation'.

Three days after reaching the town their man was located at a house in the outskirts of town—a house, as they learned, that was somewhat noted. For several years it had been suspected of being the hiding place of a gang of counterfeiters.

Now that they had located their man, it remained for them to capture him.

"How do you propose to work him, Mr. Smith?" asked Charley.

"I want to make a raid on the place—I think there's a regular gang of them here, and I want to capture all of them and their outfit too. I have arranged with the sheriff and his posse who are ready and awaiting our

(28)

In the Counterfeiter's Den.

signal. The sheriff told me that the first house was built there ten years ago. Since then it has been burned down and rebuilt three times. It is one of the oldest houses in town. The town had always been infested with burglars and counterfeiters and it was believed, that this house was their headquarters; yet it had always escaped detection. Three times it had burned down while being searched."

So, as it was all arranged, they set about watching for an opportunity to make the raid—an opportunity, which soon arrived; for that very evening the man whom they had spotted was run to the house and the signal given for the attack.

The sheriff stationed his men so that it would be impossible for anyone to make their escape from the house; and then the old man, Charley, the sheriff and his deputy approached the door and knocked.

The door opened, and a man appeared and very politely enquired their business.

''Oh!" he exclaimed, and then said politely: ''Come in, gentlemen, come in. I will render you all the aid possible."

From garret to cellar the house was searched. Not a crack nor crevice but what was pried into in hope of finding some secret passage. Twice they returned to the cellar, but all efforts to discover anything availed nothing. But Charley was not satisfied; somehow he felt that there was some secret hiding place about the house and he believed it to be in the cellar.

The cellar contained but one room—a large, square room with a chimney support in the centre, and a pile of boxes, barrels and other rubbish in one corner. There was a peculiarity about the cellar, and that was a plank floor.

"What is that floor for anyway?" mused Charley, as they left the house. "By ginger now, I don't like the result of this search a bit. Say!" he said, addressing the old man, "did you notice anything unusual about that cellar?"

"No," he replied.

"But that floor and that chimney support—"

"I examined every crack in that floor and the chimney support too," interrupted the old man.

"Well," replied Charley, "I ain't just satisfied, I would like to search that cellar again. That chimney support appears to me to offer a clue to some secret hiding place."

"I didn't notice anything peculiar about it," said the old man. "A sort of cupboard, that's all. But what do you think?" he asked, as they stopped, still within sight of the house and in a position where they could see anyone passing to or from the house.

As they were standing thus, conversing, a gentleman and lady entered the house, but no one had left it.

"Let's go and examine that cellar again," said Charley,

So back they went. The people were just as polite as before; the only difference was, there were three men and two women now instead of two men and one woman as before.

To Charley's surprise he beheld the beautiful girl whom he had met on the train. She greeted him with a look of injured surprise and reproach and, to Charley, seemed rather pale aud anxious.

Down into the cellar they went, accompanied by the three men. Everything was just as before, nothing had been disturbed.

It had been arranged that, at a signal from the old man, they were to draw their revolvers and demand the surrender of the three men and then to proceed with the search.

As they entered the cellar, the three men leading, the old man, in a stern voice, demanded the immediate surrender of the men. For a moment they hesitated, but looking into the muzzles of a half dozen revolvers, they deemed it policy to obey. They were placed in charge of two men and sent up stairs to await the result of the search.

"Now for the search!" said the old man; and he began examining the chimney support. In the examination several peculiarities were discovered. It was just the width of two planks and fitted nicely over the cracks in the floor, and was about three feet long.

Somehow the notion that there was a trap door under it had got into Cbariey's head. But all efforts to move it, failed, and to all apperances it was perfectly stationary and had never been moved.

They were about to give up again when, chancing to look up at the top of the support, Charley saw that some of the nails were not driven quite in—a very small thing, but sometimes small things lead to great results. So in this; for, hardly thinking what he was doing, Charley reached up and took hold of one of the nails—

it was perfectly loose and came out easily.   All the rest
were removed in the same way, when, to their surprise,
they found that the support moved easily.

On moving it to one side, a trap door was discovered
which raised easily, disclosing a flight of steps that led
down into a dark, narrow passage below.

Down into the passage they went, with guns in readiness, alert and careful.

A heavy plank door closed the passage, but fortunately, or rather unfortunately, it was not fastened—
strange too, but they took no further notice of it. Pushing the door open, they entered a small room where they
found all the necessary tools and fixtures of the burglars
and counterfeiter's art, together with some thousands of
dollars of counterfeit money.   But the man was not
there.

"Can it be possible that he has eluded us?" asked the
old man.   "He certainly has occupied this room, and
that too while we were searching the house.   I—"

"Listen!', whispered Charley, "I heard something; it
sounded like footsteps on the stairs."   But listening
again they heard nothing.

The old man went up to the head of the stairs, but
seeing nothing, returned and began searching the room.

"It must have been a rat," he said.   "There's no one
above; the door leading up stairs is locked, so that no
one could get out or in."

Just then he noticed a place beneath the stairs—the
only place that they had not searched, but there was no
one there, though there was plenty of room for a man
to hide.

"You are sure, are you, that there is no place above where he could have hid from you?" asked Charley.

"Yes, I am sure," replied the old man. "There was but one place and that was behind the support—I looked there."

"But the trap door, did you—"

"God!" cried the old man, as if he had been shot. "I—"

Down went the trap door with a bang and before they could reach it, the chimney support was in place and the door fastened.

"Trapped, by thunder!" ejaculated Charley, after satisfying himself that the door was immovable.

"My God," exclaimed the old man in vexation. "I never thought of that trap door! He must have been been behind it; but how did he dodge us?'

"Dodge us!" said Charley; "he was in that hole under the stairs, and while we were searching the room, he stole out. Yes, we were too anxious to find the end of the passage and thus went by his hiding place without seeing it. Oh, we are trapped all right enough."

———:o:———

CHAPTER VI.

"Well, I reckon there's nothing for it but to wait till our men above get tired of waiting for us and come down to see what's up with us. No need to feel alarmed, I think, for they'll soon begin to get uneasy about us; so we can just take our time to examine this place.

The room was small and nearly square. A few chairs, a table, a bench, forge and a complete set of burglars' tools, dies and plates for counterfeiting, together with several other articles and several bundles of counterfeit money, both paper and coin, made up the list of things found.

They saw plainly enough that their man had been concealed beneath the stairs when they came down, but in their excitement they had overlooked him.

They had almost forgotten their imprisonment, so interested were they in examining the many curious things that they found, until their attention was called to the fact by a strong smell of smoke.

"By thunder!" cried Charley, sniffing the air; and then he remembered what the sheriff had told them about how the house had been burned three times before while being searched. A startling state of affairs, to be sure; but what could be done? "What can it mean?" asked Charley.

"Mean," sputtered the old man, "it means that unless help comes pretty soon, we will be roasted alive!"

"That's what!" declared Charley. "See! the smoke is coming in through those little holes up there in the wall. I wonder if I can't stop them up and keep the

(34)

"Unless Help Comes We Will Be Roasted Alive."

smoke out. By ginger, we'll be suffocated directly!"
And climbing up to the holes, evidently used for ventila-
tion, he peered within and was horrified at seeing the
flames not far above. Burning embers began to fall
down and the roar of the flames were now plainly
heard.

In blank amazement the two men stood, staring at
each other. What could they do? Perfectly helpless,
neither could offer any suggestion. The smoke, by this
time, had become well-nigh suffocating.

"Great heavens!" cried the old man in his despair,
"is it possible that something has happened to our
friends above and we are left to perish in such a miserable trap as this? I have been in the business for fifteen
years, and in all kinds of places, but this takes the cake!
How did this all come about, anyway?"

"Oh!" they have set the house on fire to enable them
to escape," replied Charley.

"Ah! I see now," said the old man. "This place
has never been found before, or, if it has, the knowledge
of it has been buried with the unfortunate cuss who
perished here, as we will. Yes, yes; of course, when
the house burns down, the passage to this place will be
filled with ashes and no one would ever suspect that
such a place existed. But how did it happen? can it be
that our friends have deserted us? they certainly must
have discovered the fire long before this."

"No doubt, it was the man who escaped from us here.
He set fire to that pile of rubbish in the cellar—that
stuff was there for that very purpose," declared our
young friend.

"But our friends! have they deserted us?"

Just then the tramping of men was heard above, followed by shouts and blows upon the floor and walls, as if in search of some hidden passage.

Quickly ascending the stairs, the two entrapped men endeavored to make their presence known by shouting and pounding upon the trap door.

The signal was heard, for, in a moment, heavy blows sounded above and, though it seemed an age to the nearly suffocated men below, the door was hewn from its hinges and gave way.

A deluge of water poured in upon them as the door opened, for it was only by continuously throwing water upon the men, that they were enabled to work at all in the terrible heat of the fire.

The sheriff and his deputy, who were guarding the prisoners above, had not discovered the fire till it was seen from the outside and the alarm given.

The prisoners, of course, took advantage of the exitement and made their escape, so nothing remained but to take up the trail and follow them up.

The finding of the trail was not an easy matter; but, fortunately, enough was learned to convince them that their man had gone west. The old man had learned before that they operated at Bozeman as well as at Miles, and he believed that they would go there; so they decided to go to Bozeman without delay.

————:o:————

A Frightened Couple.

CHAPTER VII.

KITTY BARNES.

The journey up the river to Bozeman was a pleasant one; and the days passed so quickly that they reached their journey's end almost before they were aware of it.

They found Bozeman to be like all western frontier towns: gambling dens, saloons, and dance halls upon every hand.

Not long after reaching the city, a clew which led to the discovery of the hiding place of a regular band of outlaws was found. It happened this way:

One evening, some two days after arriving at Bozeman, Charley was walking along the street when some one called to him—

"Hellow there, old fellow," he said, "how are you?"

"All right," replied Charley dryly.

"Guess you recognize me?"

"Well no, not hardly," replied Charley, wondering what kind of a game the fellow was trying to run on him.

Don't you remember that little affair down at Miles City, where we pulled you out of that burning buildiug? I was one of them."

"No,' replied Charley, "I don't remember—guess you must be mistaken in your man—I don't remember you at any rate," thought Charley.

"Beg pardon then," said the fellow; "I thought that you were the man. Well, it's my treat—come in here and wet up a little on that," he said and led the way into a saloon.

"By thunder," mused Charley, as he followed his new

(37)

found friend into the crowded saloon, "I will see what his game is."

"Here, have a drink," said the fellow, raising his glass.

"Don't drink," said Charley.

"Smoke then?"

"Nor smoke."

"Let's have a game, then, just to pass away the time."

"I never play."

"Well, I never!" exclaimed the fellow; and turning away in disgust, at what he deemed such a verdant greenhorn, he left Charley altogether at a loss to understand what was up. But he was destined soon to learn. The fellow had played his part and now it remained for another to carry it out.

"Mr. Shipton?" and a light hand was placed upon Charley's shoulder. "Charley Shipton, I believe?" came in a low, sweet voice that trembled with some inward emotion.

"Yes," said Charley, and turning quickly to face his new enemy—for enemy he certainly must be. "Gosh!" he exclaimed, as his gaze rested upon the pale, beautiful face of his former companion upon the train; the same that he had seen at the house in Miles City. "Beg pardon," he said, and held out his hand to her.

"Is your name Charley Shipton, sir?" she asked, placing her little, soft hand in his broad, brown palm.

"Yes," answered Charley. "Didn't I tell you my name that night on the train?"

"No," she answered, "I wouldn't tell you mine, so

you wouldn't tell me yours. But here's a note." And she placed a piece of paper in his hand.

The note read: "Friend Charley.—Come to me quick; I am in trouble and must have help. I have located our man. I send this by Kitty, the saloon girl. Follow her and she will show you the way—"

"Who gave you this?" asked Charley.

"I don't know," she answered evasively.

"Where is he?"

"Come with me, and I will show you."

"No, you must tell me first."

"He is back in the distillery."

"Distillery—"

"Sh— some one might hear you. Come with me," she said anxiously.

"All right! Let's get out of here, I want to talk with you."

"Follow me then." And she led the way toward the door in the rear end of the saloon.

"Not that way," said Charley.

"Yes, yes, come along; we can't go out the front door, some one is watching us."

"They can't stop us!" said Charley, with a frown.

"But they can stop me," replied the girl anxiously.

"No—"

"Yes, they can," interrupted the girl. "My father and brother are here; come on, please, I want to tell you something."

"But won't they follow us?"

"Not for a little while; come with me and I will tell you just as soon as we are out of sight." And she led the way to the door.

No one seemed to take any especial notice of them, as they passed out of the hall and closed the door behind them. Here Charley found himself in a large dance hall. Though it was early, a few couples had already entered the hall, and were strolling about or sitting, chatting with one another.

"We will wait till the dance begins," said the girl, "and then we will go."

"But you can tell me your story; no one will hear us here," said Charley.

"Yes, but let's go and sit down over there by that door first; we will have to go out there. But I want to ask you a few questions first."

"Well, I am in for it now, so fire away."

"Do you drink?"

"No."

"Don't play cards or gamble?"

"No."

"Are you a detective?"

He hesitated.

"I am only a girl. Are you afraid to answer me?"

"No, not afraid!"

"Are you a detective?" she asked, and her wide, blue eyes looked up into his with such a pleading look that he could not refuse.

"Yes," he answered, "but I am not in the service now—I am off on a summer's vacation. But why do you ask?"

"My brother keeps this house; my father owned that house that was burned down at Miles City, and it was my brother that you were after there. You have followed us here to capture my father and two brothers, and take them off to prison. No doubt, you think they are bad people; they never injured you—they did, what they did, to defend themselves; they are compelled to defend themselves again and against you. I have led you here at their command; my father wrote that note and commanded me to do what I have done. Your friend, the detective, was trapped the same way, and he is back in the still-room, now, a prisoner. My father and two brothers are in the saloon there and saw me when I brought you here. You could not get away from here, if you were to try."

"Now, I will tell you why I asked you these questions —I did it, to see, if I could trust you."

"But how can you tell by that?" asked Charley.

"I wouldn't trust a man that drinks or gambles," she replied warmly.

"Well?" said Charley inquiringly.

"To use a gambler's phrase, I am playing a desperate game; but I hold the trumps—I want you to promise me that you will let my people alone. If you will do this, I will get you out of here; if you refuse, then you are a doomed man!"

"But the detective, I can't leave him here alone?"

"He can escape the same way; we will take him with us."—

"But you may not be able to do this, my little friend," said Charley.

"I may not be able to save you! But here comes the dancers—you will have to decide quick."

"I'll promise."

"All right.   Do you dance."

"No," replied Charley.

"Well, you can try anyhow.   Let's go around a time, then we will go."

And they joined the merry throng of dancers and went whirling around the room.   As they came to the door, his companion said, nervously:

"Here, come quick!"

And stepping through the door, they found them-selves in a dark passage, through which they groped their way back into a large store-room.   The door and windows were barred, so that escape would be impos-sible.

At a glance he saw how completely he had been trapped, for that was a part of the game.   She was to lead him there with the hope of escape.

"By ginger," cried Charley, I am trapped."

"No, no," said the girl, "trust to me, I will save you yet.   I had to bring you here, this is a part of the game; but you shall see that I am an honest girl."

Already, back in the dark passage, through which they came, the heavy footsteps of men were heard approaching.

"Here, quick," said the girl, "get under this empty hogshead; they won't find us here, I have hid here before!"

Hardly had they concealed themselves, when two men entered the room in search of them.

"I don't believe that they came here," said one of them.

"But I saw them in the hall and I know, that they didn't go back into the saloon," replied the other.

"One of them, leaning against the hogshead, under which the fugitives were concealed, said:

"I'll tell you what it is, Dick, I don't believe that that girl can be trusted—she's too much like mother used to be."

"I don't know," replied the other, "she trapped the old man all right."

"Yes. that was all right, but she's a little struck on that young fellow. Deuced fine-looking fellow he is too, I don't know as I blame the girl much, after all. We had no business to force this upon her."

"Don't fool yourself, we couldn't manage him any other way. Perhaps she couldn't get him to come here,"

Just then two more men entered.

"Its my father, two brothers, and uncle Dick," whispered the girl. "Oh, if they should find us!"

"He has escaped," said the man that was leaning against their hiding place.

"Impossible!" cried one, he couldn't get out of this house."

"Where's Kitty?" demanded another, evidently her father.

"Two of you go on into the still-room, and we will go back and see if any one has seen them," said some one.

"Good!" whispered the girl with a sigh of relief.

Presently the two men returned from the still-room, and a moment later, Charley and his companion heard the door of the store-room close behind them.

"Come now," said the girl, "we have no time to

lose." And crawling from their hiding place, they
stood in the dim light of the store-room.

No avenue of escape could be seen; nothing but solid
walls, barred doors and windows. But the girl was
equal to the occasion; for, going up to one side of the
room, to what appeared to be an old mantlepiece, she
pressed upon a hidden spring—the mantle swung open,
and she motioned Charley to enter and, quickly following, she closed the mantle behind her.

"Come," she said, "give me your hand."

"Yes, and my heart too, little girl, if you want it,"
said Charley.

"You had better save it, you may need it yourself,'
she replied, as she led him through a passage, dark as
Egypt. "Be careful now." And down a flight of stairs
they went.

The way was long and steep and so narrow, that
Charley's broad shoulders were continually rubbing against
the walls upon either side.

Down, down, groping their way in the darkness, far
below the level of the ground where, at last, they stopped
before a door—the door to the still-room.

Slipping back the heavy bolts which fastened the
door, they entered the room. All was still as the tomb,
and the darkness was so intense that they could almost
feel it.

"I wonder what this means?" murmured the girl. "It
must be that they have taken him away."

"Perhaps not," said Charley, "he may be asleep."

"Have you got a match?" she asked.

"Yes, I always carry matches," answered Charley.
And producing one, he lit it.

"There is a lamp here—ah, here it is," said the girl; and she lit it.

By the dim, flickering light, Charley saw that he was in a small room, surrounded by barrels and kegs. In one corner was an arch and still, but there was no one in the room.

Looking into the pale face of his little companion, Charley saw that she was troubled and frightened.

"Kitty—" it was the first time he had taken the liberty of addressing her thus—"what do you think?"

"I don't know, I am afraid that we are trapped," she answered.

"But what did you bring me here for?" asked Charley rather reproachfully.

"To get your friend. I thought that we would find him here; he was here, not more than two hours ago," answered the girl, tearfully.

"Are you sure of that?"

"Yes, he ought to be here now."

"Could he escape?"

"No; they have taken him away."

"Where would they take him?"

"Oh, I don't know," said the girl with a shudder.

"If they have murdered him, they shall suffer for it!" exclaimed Charley, angrily.

"You may suffer the same fate. You couldn't escape from this room, if you were to try."

He saw at a glance that her words were only too true. He would have to go back the way they came and discovery would inevitably follow the attempt.

"There's but one hope now—I must hide you here and wait for an opportunity to get you away. But you have got to make me a promise first. You must promise me that you will leave this place alone and not trouble us any more."

"But my friend, Kitty, what about him?"

"I don't know. I can answer nothing of him. If they have put him out of the way, they did it to protect themselves—you would do the same thing."

"But I will avenge his death—I will punish his murderers!"

"You will have to escape first."

"No, you are in my power—I can begin here. I am armed, I can wait till they come here and then I can shoot two or three of them, at least."

"That would do you no good. There are twenty men here—you can't kill them all. But, if you want to try it, kill me first, Charley."

"Kill you! my dear, little girl! do you think I would harm you?" he asked; and he looked down into her beautiful, wondering eyes with such a reproachful look.

"But you think that I have deceived you! Oh! Charley! I am honest in this—I have done the best I could—"

"Hark! did you hear that?" asked Charley.

"No, I didn't hear anything," she said, cowering close to his side, trembling with fear.

"There it is again!"

"They are coming—quick, follow me!" And blowing out the light, she grasped his hand and led him to the still and whispered—

"Crawl in there."

It was rather a disagreeable place, but they thought nothing of that; so into the arch they crawled, where they waited in breatless silence.

Presently the heavy door opened, and the men entered the room.

"They are here—they must be," said one. "I left the door bolted; none else has been here!"

"They are not here now—they must have gone back,' said another.

"That's impossible," said a third, "you must be mistaken about bolting the door. The girl knows nothing about the secret passage that leads up the chimney."

Charley felt the little form at his side quiver with excitement, as the man mentioned the secret passage.

Every corner of the room was searched; every box and barrel was looked into in the hope of finding the fugitives. Once, one of the men came and peered into the arch. Down upon his knees, his head thrust half way through the doorway, he peered long and steadily, and, it seemed to the fugitives, directly at them. The little form at Charley's side shrunk and quivered with despair. No pen could portray the agony of feeling at the thought that they were discovered. The least sign upon the part of the man, showing that he had discovered them, would have sealed his doom.

, 'Well, they are not here, that's certain," said the man, drawing his head from the arch and rising to his feet.

"There's a traitor in camp!" exclaimed another. "Someone has told him of the plot, and he has made his escape and kidnapped the girl too."

"Well, let's go back and report."

And in a moment more they had left the room, taking the lamp with them and bolting the door on the outside.

Crawling from their hiding place, they went to the door and listened, till they were satisfied that the men were gone. Then lighting a match, they searched for the lamp, but, to their dismay, found, that the men had taken it with them.

Trying the door, they found, that it was bolted fast— no hope of escape there.

Next, the secret passage in the chimney, but it was utterly impossible to find it.

Discouraged and hopeless, they sat down together in the darkness. Despair had driven the last ray of hope from the girl's heart. Weary and discouraged they sat in gloomy silence. A slight noise fell upon their ears. With bated breath they listened.

A door in one side of the room creaked upon its hinges and a heavy footstep sounded upon the floor. Then a silence, deep as death, pervaded the room. The seconds seemed to drag themselves into hours; still no sound. Could it have been the imagination of a fevered brain?

No—again came the sound of that step, cautiously and stealthily, approached them.

Nearer and nearer it came.

Trembling with terror, the poor girl! crouched close to her companion's side. In the awful, silent darkness, the slow, cautious approach of that unseen visitor was enough to strike terror to a stronger heart than hers.

On it came, till now, it stood by Charley's side; then, for an instand, it paused. So close was it, that its garments touched those of the crouching fugitives. Then, silent as before, it moved to the other side of the room.

"Come," whispered Charley, grasping his companion's arm. And, as silent as the unseen figure, they glided quickly across the room to the open door, through which the stranger had entered; they stepped within, closed the door and bolted it fast.

Looking up, they could see the twinkling stars above them; and they knew, from what they had heard, that they were in the chimney. Pins upon one side of the chimney, served as a ladder, and they were not slow to take the hint.

Availing themselves of this avenue of escape, they soon had the pleasure and gratification of finding themselves in the open air, standing upon the flat roof of the building.

A fire escape led from this to a lower roof and then to the ground.

Not till they had reached the ground did they feel safe.

"Well," said Charley, "we are safe now; now then, the next question is, what will you do? I can't leave you unprotected—you have been faithful to me, Kitty, and I will stand by you."

"I have done this for my father," she said, "remember your promise."

"But you, Kitty?"

"Never mind me, Charley, I can take care of myself," she answered.

"But I can't leave you here."

"It wouldn't be safe for you to be seen here with me, so leave me. I have nothing to fear—I will tell father all about it; he will take care of me."

"But the old man—what of him?" asked Charley.

"I know nothing about him, Charley."

"I must find him—I can't leave a friend that way. If they have murdered him, they shall suffer for it."

"You owe your life to me, Charley; just a word from me would have sealed your doom."

"Dou you want me, Kitty?"

"I don't feel like joking, Charley," she replied, reproachfully.

"But I am in earnest, Kitty—it's all I have to give."

"Will you give me what I ask?"

"Yes, what is it?"

"That you will promise to let us alone."

"Do you want me to go away?"

"O no, I didn't say that," she answered quickly.

"But my friend, Kitty, I can't leave him. I will never leave a friend to save myself, never!"

"Neither will I!" said Kitty petulantly. My father is my friend, and I will fight for him—"

"He isn't as good a friend to you as he ought to be—"

"Stop!" cried Kitty, "I wont hear it!"

"Shake hands, Kitty, and make up—let's be friends in spite of all. You help me and I will help you!"

"O Charley, I thank you, indeed I do! I will go and try what I can do for your friend. Meet me here to-morrow night, and I will tell you what I can do for him."

"'Nough said, Kitty, I'll do it." And so they parted.

"You Have Deceived me, Charley."

CHAPTER VIII.

KITTY WINS.

The next morning Charley set out to keep his appointment with his little friend, and arriving at the appointed place, found her already there and waiting.

"Well," said Charley, "you have kept your promise, I see."

"Yes," she answered, "didn't you expect it?"

"O yes, of course I did."

"Well, come with me, I want to talk with you, and I would rather find a more comfortable place than this."

"Where shall we go?" asked Charley.

"Oh, let's walk down by the brook—we can talk as we go."

"Have you learned anything of my friend?"

"Yes, but you will have to let me tell my story in my own way—I always have my own way."

"Well, you can't always have your own way—but go ahead and tell your story."

"My brother is innocent—"

"Innocent! interrupted Charley, "innocent of what?"

"Of the crime that he's accused of—the crime that you are hunting him for!"

"Well?" said Charley interrogatively.

"My brother was a cashier in a bank; he had an enemy—a rival—some love affair, of course. This rival was a clerk in the same bank, with my brother. The bank was robbed and this fellow was killed. Suspicion pointed to my brother as the murderer; his friends turned against him; discouraged and disheartened, he fled; but he was innocent of the crime. My father was a merchant in Cincinnati; but through the treachery of supposed friends he was led into a transaction that ruined him. He and I went to Miles City, where he engaged to a company as an engraver. You broke up the business there, and we came here where my oldest brother has been in business for nearly five years."

"A queer kind of business for an honest man to fol-low," ventured Charley.

"My brother is an engraver and he's working for a company—the same company that my father was work-ing for—he has nothing to do with the business of that house," she said

"He's guilty just the same!" declared Charley.

"I don't believe it!" cried the girl.

"Besides he has attempted my life—perhaps has, already, taken the life of my friend."

"They did it in self-defence!"

"That don't lessen the crime."

"But your friend is not dead!"

"So much the better for your people — where is he?"

"He's here. "

"Here! You remember what I told you—that I would give you till to-night to release my friend—"

"You never told me any such thing, nor would I have done it if you had! I promised to meet you and tell you what I could do."

"Well, tell me that."

"I have a proposition to make; but first, who is the

best friend to you, and who do you like the best, me or the old man? Which one of us do you prefer? Choose now; you can't have us both!"

"Kitty, what do mean by this? What kind of a game are you trying to play on me?" demanded Charley, seizing the girl's little hands and looking down into her frightened, wondering eyes.

"Take your choice," she cried desperately; "shall it be me or him?"

"I don't understand just what you mean, Kitty. Tell me just what you want, Kitty."

"I want you to let my father and brothers alone—that's all I ask."

"I will never do that!" cried he, "I will raid the place this very night!"

"Then you don't want me for a friend—you have deceived me, Charley."

"I didn't say that, nor I didn't mean it! We will always be friends, Kitty—we can't be otherwise. But the old man must be given up—they must release him."

"That they will never do. But if you will see my father, you can save—"

"Kitty, this is a scheme to trap me! you are working under your father's orders—you are more dangerous to me than all the rest together! I will give them just two hours to release my friend !"

"They will never do it!"

"Then down they go!"

"You sign your friend's death warrant!"

"And they sign theirs."

"No sir, we can make our escape—we have other

places to go to; I can give the warning and before you can raise a force, we will away!"

"But I won't let you do it—I will keep you with me!"

"You can't do it!"

"Can't! Pooh, little girl! I can take you under my arm and carry you home with me."

"Will you do it?"

"Of course I will."

"Take me then!" And she raised her tearful eyes to his. "Take me, Charley, I am your prisoner."

"I will tell you, Kitty, what I'll do—you go back and tell your people to release the detective on his and their own terms. I will accept them. **The responsibility will rest with them.**"

"All right, I will do it!"

"I shall expect him by morning."

"You will wait till then?"

"Yes, but no longer."

"Probably we will never meet again, so good-bye, Charley."

"No, I won't say good-bye, Kitty, we won't part like this—"

"It's your own choice, Charley, you choose between us—"

"Kitty, you shall not drive me away so—we will be friends!"

"You can't be a friend to a counterfeiter's daughter—you have chosen—"

"I tell you I have done no such a thing, but if you want to force this on me—if you don't want my friendship, all right; but don't lay it to me."

"I made you a fair offer,—you chose him—"

"I never did it—I won't do it—I'll take it back!" cried Charley. "I would rather have you than a dozen old men!"

"Then you trust this to me. I will promise you that your friend shall go free if he will leave the country."

"I have no doubt but what he will be only too glad to do that."

"Will you let me go home now, Charley? It's getting late and father will think that you have carried me off."

"Yes, you may go, but remember, Kitty, we are to be the very best of friends—we will meet again."

"I hope so—good-bye."

At daylight the next morning the old man was released and a few hours later started for Cincinuati, leaving Charley to pursue his course alone.

During the day, Charley met Kitty and told her of his plan—how he proposed to spend his "Summer's Vacation."

"I will meet you again, Kitty, so good-bye for a while."

———:o:——— .

CHAPTER IX.

THE DEVIL'S CANON.

The next day Charley met an old man—an old California miner and prospecter—who was just ready for a prospecting trip into the mountains. And after a little talk it was arranged that Charley should accompany him.

This change in Charley's plan was owing to the stories told of a wonderful and mysterious place called "The Devil's Canon." Such wild and almost incredible stories were told of that, had it not been that the old man had been there and seen it, Charley would have discredited the whole thing as a myth. But as it was, though he had no faith in it, he determined to go; and less than two hours afterwards, was on the road.

The journey up the river was pleasant. Beautiful scenery, varied by hill and plain, back of which towered the now snow capped mountains and dark evergreen forests, lent a charm to the scene that would tax the imagination of a poet to portray.

Ten days after leaving Bozeman, they reached their destination.

The place selected for their camp was in a deep, sheltered canon, surrounded by dense forests and rugged mountains, high and steep.

"I was here last fall," said the old man, "and this is the place I selected for my campin' place.

"And this is the 'Devil's Canon then, is it?" asked Charley, a little disappointed.

"No," replied the old man," ther 'Devil's Canon' is jest over yon range ov mount'ns."

(56)

THE DEVIL'S CANON.

"But I thought that we were to camp there," said Charley.

"Not hardly! I wouldn't care to camp thar."

"Why?"

"Well," replied the old man, you'll find out soon enough."

"I am not superstitious."

"That's all right! but I want to tell ye, I've tramped these mountains nigh on to forty year, an' them that knew old Jack, don't call him a coward."

"Well, if it's such a mysterious and unearthly place, with goblins and phantoms, we would be in no danger of interferance from any one else," suggested Charley.

"Thar's jest whar you'r off," replied old Jack. "If we could have it all to ourselves, we could make our fortunes shortly.

"But who will interfere?"

"I can't tell that," replied Jack.

"You imagine somebody would?"

"I know it."

"But you don't know whether it be man, beast or devil."

"Nary one."

Not being able to find out anything, Charley concluded to investigate the matter for himself.

The first few days were devoted to preparing a comfortable camp, as they intended to stay for several weeks.

This done they set about prospecting the surrounding country. As the old man showed no disposition to go to the "Devil's Canon", Charley concluded to pay it a visit by himself.

"It's my opin' you'll not tarry thar long," said Jack. "Thar's strange goin's on do happen thar sometimes."

"You have been there, then, have you?" asked Charley.

"Yes, once."

"Won't you go again?"

"Not while I know myself," he replied.

"Jack," said Charley, "you are too old to be duped by any such nonsense   It's nothing but an Indian tradition that gave the place its name.   There's nothing unnatural, unearthly nor devilish about it.   Fancy has peopled it with demons, goblins and the ghosts of supposed victims—"

"Look a here, Charley, I'll tell you a story about that place if you want to hear it."

"That's just what I want."

"In forty-nine, me an' my pard, we went into the mines in California.   But, like most all, we wasn't successful, so we went to prospectin'.   For weeks and months we tramped about without seein' a single soul. We wandered over into this part of the country, somewhere here-abouts.   One day, while out huntin', we got after a bar.   I got a shot at him and crippled him; we trailed him through the woods for a considerabl distance, when he went down into one of the worst canons I ever seen.   Thar's something unearthly about that place, but what it was, I couldn't tell.   Finally the bar went into a cave—

" 'Jack!' " said my pard, " 'is there anything the matter with me?' "

"I looked at him; he was pale as death an' trembling, an' great drops of perspiration out on his face.   Just

then a low moaning sound fell upon my ears an' a feeling as if something, some unearthly thing was reaching
out behind me an' a trying to take a hold of me, came
over me."

" 'What is it—what's the matter?'" said my pard.

"It's the bar a-groaning," I said; but I didn't believe
it. Come on, I said, "let's go in an' drag him out.

"We entered the cave by creeping through a long,
narrow passage. It was as light in there as day, but
where the light came from I could never tell. O what
a sight met our eyes! As far as we could see, gleaming
pillars of quartz and glittering stalactites dazzled our
eyes. Peal upon peal of thunder rolled up from away
down below. Then moanin', sighin', and finally breaking out into the most unearthly shriek I ever heard.

"Everywhere we could see the glitter of gold. We
thought no more of fhe bear; but recovering from our
surprise a little, we began to look about us. Right at
my feet I saw the largest nugget of gold I ever saw—I
stooped to pick it up. At the same time my pard stepped forward; and again the cave was filled with that
awful shriek; bewildered and terror-stricken, I dropped
the nugget and raised up—I was alone; and from that
day to this, I never saw nor heard of my pard."

"And do you think that that cave is in 'Devil's Canon?'
asked Charley.

"I left that place an' went back to California, but the
memory of that awful place and the mysterious disappearance of my pard haunted me day and night, till I
made up my mind to go back.

"For years I have tramped these mountains, but not
till last fall could I find a trace of the place; or any place

that appeared to answer the description of it."

"And you think that this is the place, do you?" asked Charley.

"Yes, I found our old camp."

"What do you suppose became of your friend?"

"I don't know."

"What do you think causes the mystery of that place?"

"I don't know; but since I came here I have seen some queer things.—I was standing, one day, beside a hole in the ground that looked like a large well, when, all of a sudden, up, out of that hole, went a column of boilin' hot water and mud for a hundred feet or more, then fell back with an awful roar."

"Do you attribute the sounds in the cave to the same cause?"

"It may be; but where did my pard go to? and what caused that awful, queer feelin' to come over me and take my strength away?"

"There's some mystery, perhaps some electrical phenomena connected with the place."

"Would that have such an effect?"

"Yes."

"The Indians say that no man can go there and return again. Prisoner and criminals, that are condemned to die, are sent there and never return."

"But how about you? you say that you have been there."

"Well, in my case it don't fit; but in my pards, it does."

"I am a-going to see that place before I leave here — will you show me the way?" asked Charley.

"I will show you the place, but I won't go in."

Early the next morning Charley was calculating to go, but, before starting, three men came into camp, so he postponed going.

That evening they were speaking of the place, when all three of the men declared their intention of visiting it the next day, if old Jack would show them the way.

"All right, boys," said old Jack.

Bright and early the next morning they started.

About three miles from camp, they found the trail that led to the canon. It was the only place that one could enter "that land from whence no traveler returns."

"You can't miss the way," said old Jack, "keep right ahead for about a quarter of a mile an' you'll come out into the canon. In the middle of the place is a round lake, an' a little to the right is the cave."

"All right, boys," said one as they disappeared.

"Come on, pilgrim," said Jack, "I want to show you something."

Turning to the left they walked rapidly, climbing up the steep sides of the mountains, till they came out on the verge of a high precipice, overlooking what appeared to be a large, round hole in the earth. It was nearly a quarter of a mile across each way, with perpendicular walls fully a quarter of a mile in depth, and unbroken, except for one place. That was the dark, narrow defile which they had just left.

It was a grand and awful sight. Not a living thing could be found within the pale of those circular walls; not a tree, not even a little shrub.

In the center was a circular basin of water, or rather of mud.

"That lake is, so the Indians say, a lake of fire where the spirits of the victims of this death hole dwell," said old Jack. "Hark!" he whispered, "did you hear that?"

"I heard the wind," said Charley.

"Wind!" said Jack contemptuously. "The wind don't make no such noise as that!"

"It's thunder."

"Thunder don't come from the ground, does it?"

"Look!" said Charley, "there are the men, now."

"They are afraid to go; I can tell by their actions!" exclaimed Jack.

"But they are going. Ah, they have reached the cave and are entering."

"If they enter, then we will never see them again," said Jack with a shudder. And he turned away, muttering: "Gone—gone."

The minutes lapsed into hours, still they did not return. The sun sunk behind the western hills and darkness closed down around them, still they watched and waited for the strangers, but they never returned.

But now that darkness had come, a new phenomena was revealed. Pale lights and tongues of flame shot up from the lake and flitted about over its surface, assuming all imaginable forms. No wonder the Indians and superstitious hunters looked upon it with a feeling of dread. All manner of sounds came floating up to them, and, a very easy matter indeed would it be for the ears of the superstitious to hear the groans and cries of lost spirits mingling with the hellish laughter of devils and demons.

"Jack, this abode of devils is nothing more nor less

than a giant geyser," said Charley. "You have seen the same things in the National Park. That lake of fire is a boiling caldron of mud and water, and those lights and flames and imaginary forms are nothing but gas escaping, and that too is causing the noise we hear."

"That may be, and I believe it is; but what is the cause of the death of men and animals that go there?" asked Jack.

"I don't know," answered Charley, "but I would like to investigate it and see."

"Well, let's go home," said Jack.

And with a feeling of relief he led the way back to camp.

—:o:—

CHAPTER X.

THE CRAZY HERMIT.

Two days after the disappearance of the three men, who had entered the cave, a large band of Indians camped a little below our friends; so they deemed it prudent to move. They went around to the other side of the canon and went into camp there.

One day, shortly after this, as Charley was going along a little stream, he discovered the bare-foot tracks of a man in the sand; calling Jack's attention to it, he answered:

"There's a story told of an old man that lives somewhere in these mountains and, as the story goes, he found a great nugget of gold—the largest that was ever found in California. It was stolen from him, but he trailed the thieves for days and weeks, and finally came upon them in their camp. Pretending to be lost, he begged them to let him stay over night with them. In the night, when they were asleep, he arose, and put poison in the coffee pot and then lay down and waited. In the morning, not wishing to intrude too much upon their hospitality, he departed before breakfast. When he thought that all would be over, he went back, and found the three men helpless, but not dead. He went and got the nugget, then going up to one of them, he beat him with the precious stone till he was dead; and so he served the other two.

"The awful crime he had committed haunted him till he lost his reason and wandered away to these mountains, where he has hid himself and his nugget ever since."

(64)

PURSUED BY INDIANS.

"Do you think that this may be his track?" asked Charley.

"More likely to be his than any one else's. I have seen this same track many times before, but I never could get to see him."

"Do you suppose that he still keeps the nugget?"

"Yes."

"If he is here, we can find him."

"I don't know, he has been hunted year after year, but has never been found yet?"

"How many years has he been here?" asked Charley.

"About twenty."

"Do you know, or did you ever hear of any one else that is living anywhere in these mountains?"

"Yes. There's an old man living in the mountains somewhere to the west of here."

"Do you know where he came from?"

"No."

"Well, we will try and find this fellow that made these tracks.

The next day they began prospecting and for two days nothing was seen of the "Old Man of the Mountains", as he was called.

On the third day Charley was out hunting, and as he was going along a deep, narrow ravine, he found the bare-foot tracks again. He knew by the looks of them that the person had just passed along and could not be more than a hundred yards away. Following for some fifty yards, he came to a dense thicket. Behind it a perpendicular wall rose to several hundred feet in heighth.

This cliff extended around in such a manner that he knew, the man who had made the tracks, must be in the thicket, for he could not possibly escape without scaling the cliff—a thing that no one could do.

Following the tracks a little farther along the edge of the ticket, he came to a little brook that led out from the thicket. The tracks entered the stream and were lost. But he must have gone up the stream, for, if he had gone the other way, he would have met Charley as he went up; so Charley followed the stream by wading till he came to the cliff. The water had gradually grown deeper and deeper, till it, at last, had reached his chin.

"Well." he mused, "he couldn't have come this way; he couldn't get out on either side, he couldn't climb the cliff, and he could— Ah, I don't know about that either! The stream comes right out from under the wall. perhaps he could go in there. This may be the entrance to a cave. But I don't believe I will try it alone. No, I'll go back and get Jack, and then we will explore this place."

The next day he started out in company with Jack; but he found to his surprise, that he could not locate the place, nor could he find a trace of it.

"It's too bad," said Jack, "that you didn't mark your trail so you could return; for, I believe that that's where he lives. If we could find him, we would make our fortunes."

Three days after this, while prospecting in a rocky gorge, Charley chanced to look down the gorge and there, not a hundred yards off, he saw a score or more of Indians, coming directly toward him.

"By ginger," he muttered, "what will I do now?"

But Charley was never long at a loss what to do. The Indians had not yet seen him; and dodging quickly out of sight, he ran up the gorge. But he had not gone far, when he was discovered.

Dashing on up the gorge, hotly pursued by the Indians, he soon came to what, to all appearances, was the end of the gorge. Perpendicular walls rose for hundreds of feet upon either side and in front.

Already the voices of his pursuers were heard, fast approaching from behind.

Running along the foot of the cliff, he soon came to a dense thicket, in which he concealed himself. In a moment more the Indians had reached and surrounded the thicket. Behind him rose the cliff wall, upon either hand, creeping closer and closer, came the eagle-eyed savages At his feet rushed the little stream from its unknown source.

To tell the thoughts which crowded through his mind would be impossible. Stories of captivity, of torture and perhaps death, loomed up before him.

"By thunder," he mused, "there's but one thing for me to do, and that is to fight! Hang me for a fool, now, if I don't make them pay for all the fun they get out of me!"

Closer and closer came the narrowing circle of savages. The shadows of evening were fast closing around them, and all was as still as death.

Nearer and nearer—now a slight rustling sound sounded ominously near.

Waiting and watching, as a cat watching for its prey, he waited, rifle in hand. A slight movement of the bushes, a dark, shadowy form, and he knew that the critical moment had arrived.

Raisiug his rifle slowly, carefully, he glanced along its deadly length, his finger touched the trigger, and—

Just at that momeut a pale, lurid light illuminated the gorge, followed by the most unearthly shriek that mortal ears ever heard. Shriek after shriek echoed aud re-echoed among the hills, till it seemed a thousand demons had joined in the hellish chorus.

Upon the opposite wall shadowy figures flitted about or engaged in endless combat, accompanied all the while by that awful shriek and demonical laughter.

Above the din, loud and clear, rang out the horrified cries of the savages, as they rushed pell-mell down the gorge.

As they fled, the figure of a man, or demon, rushed by the bewildered fugitive and disappeared in full pursuit of the terror-stricken savages, uttering all the while that awful cry.

Springing to his feet, Charley followed after him. On gainiug the other side of the gorge, he stopped upon the bank of a little stream—the same one he had found and entered a few days before, while following the barefoot tracks. On looking up to the opposite wall, he discovered the source of the pale light that lit up the scene.

It came from an opening some half-way up in the wall; but what caused it, he could not tell; nor what caused the shadowy figures on the opposite wall, though he could see that they were reflected from within the cave.

He was wondering at the strange phenomena, when a heavy step sounded behind him. On turning, he beheld a sight that, though he might live a hundred years, he will never forget. A man, fully seven feet in heighth. broad-shouldered and heavy, a veritable giant, muscular and active, with hair and beard reaching to his middle, and with that wild, unnatural look, seen only in the most dangerous maniacs. He was armed with a huge, knotted club, that would have taxed the strength of a common man to carry; which he twisted about his head as if it were but a feather.

Advancing step by step, beating his broad chest with his huge fist, as does the gorilla, all the while, uttering that demon shriek and hellish laughter, which had made him such an object of terror to those who had seen him.

Nearer and nearer he came. For a few moments, Charley stood, fascinated by the wild, strange creature, demon or devil, as he might be. But it was for a moment only. Seeing and realizing his danger, he gazed fearlessly into the gleaming eyes of the monster, and with a contemptuous smile, without a word, raised his deadly rifle, and brought it on a level with the broad chest of his adversary.

Crazy, as he was, the maniac had sense enough to know what his danger was; and seeing no trace of fear in the flashing eye that glanced along that rifle barrel, nor tremor in the hand that held it, he changed his mind, and, instead of attacklng the bold hunter, he stood for a moment in silence, and then turned and bounded away so quickly, that Charley could hardly tell which way he went.

With a feeling of relief, Charley turned and walked rapidly down the gorge; but it was so late and getting so dark, that he concluded that he could not reach camp that night, so he hunted up as comfortable a place as possible and camped down for the night.

Fortunate indeed was it for him that he did so.

——:o:——

DEATH OF JACK.

CHAPTER XI.

DEATH OF JACK.

Early the next morning Charley returned to camp. And, oh, what a sight did he behold! Lying upon the ground, in front of the little cabin, was poor, old Jack. A half dozen Indian arrows were sticking in his broad chest, while his body was horribly mutilated.

"Great God!" cried Charley, standing over the dead body, "I would like to avenge this deed. Oh, you blood-thirsty devils! Ah, I believe that it was the same outfit that was after me."

Examining the premises, Charley found, that the Indians had taken or destroyed everything. Not a thing was left. Blankets, bedding, cooking utensils, provisions and horses—all, all gone.

An indescribable feeling of loneliness came over him; and seating himself upon a seat before the cabin door, he buried his face in his hands and for a few minutes was lost in thought.

"Yes, yes," he murmured, "I will do it!" And going to his dead companion he dragged him within the cabin; closing the door, he set fire to it and retired for a little distance where he stood leaning upon his gun, and watched the funeral pyre.

In a few minutes the little cabin with its lone occupant were reduced to ashes. Then, sadly and with a heavy heart, Charley turned and hastened away, in the direction of the nearest settlement, some thirty miles away.

Hastening along through the dense forests and mountains as rapidly as possible, he came out, along toward
evening, upon a high ridge, overlooking a broad, level
valley half mile away, where he sat down to rest.

A beautiful panorama was spread before him, the
little park or valley, surrounded upon all sides by high,
snow-capped mountains and dark, dreary forests, presented the appearance, almost, of a garden in the
wilderness—an oasis in the desert.

Beautiful and peaceful was the scene, yet, so soon to
become the areua in which a bloody tragedy was to be
enacted.

Sitting thus, thinking of the sad fate of poor, old Jack
and the strange creature, whom he had met, when, from
afar down the valley, a chorus of wild yells attracted his
attention. Presently a horseman came into view, closely
followed by a half dozen Indians.

It was an exciting race; hard pressed, though the white
man was, he held his own, until he had reached a point
directly opposite of the lone spectator. The fugitive's
horse was about winded; he could not hold out much
longer, and Charley knew that he was about to witness
a bloody and exciting tragedy. How would it end? One
man against six—a one-sided combat, indeed. But,
with all the odds against him, the man was as cool and
unconcerned as if engaged in some peaceful and amusing
sport.

He had turned his flagging horse directly toward the
place where Charley stood, but it was evident that he
could not reach the shelter of the wood.

Now, with a wild yell of triumph, the savages clashed

forward, discharging a volley of bullets and arrows. Rider and horse went down in a heap. Again and again rang out that wild war-whoop, as the triumphant savages rushed upon their fallen victim.

But the tragedy was just to begin; for, as the unsuspecting savages rushed upon him to scalp him, totally unprepared for such a reception, the fallen man sprang to his feet, a revolver in either hand, and, before the Indians had time to recover from their surprise, four shots rang out, and four savages fell from their horses. The other two turned and, putting spurs to their horses, endeavored to escape; but it was too late, for, picking up his Winchester, he dropped them both before they could get out of reach.

One of the horses, freed from its rider, had fled away toward the timber below, and, thinking perhaps, that he might capture him, Charley followed after. and soon came upon him.

"By Jinks," exclaimed Charley, as he came up to the horse, "it's my own Fanny!" And calling him by name, the horse allowed himself to be caught.

Fortunate, indeed, was this for Charley, as we shall presently see.

"Ah," said Charley, patting his horse upon the neck. "fortunate for me that I found you, old fellow! I've nearly worn my legs off to-day. By jingoes though," he exclaimed, "but that was a cute trick that fellow played! Zounds, but didn't he lay 'em out cool!"

———:o:———

CHAPTER XII.

A RACE FOR LIFE.

As Charley was riding down the valley, and some ten miles from the settlement, he heard the clatter of horses hoofs sounding out behind him.   Presently some fifteen or twenty Indians came in sight.   They were on his trail and, of course, saw him as soon as he did them.

Then commenced another race, a race more exciting to Charley, at least, than the first one had been.

On, on they flew, pursued and pursuers, down the valley.   Now dashing headlong through the open, then darting among the trees, leaping fallen trees and stones, then leaping some water-worn gulley, but still pressing on in that mad race for life.

Thundering down the valley, not two hundred yards apart, horses and riders flaked with foam, they dashed. The sun had already gone down behind the western hills and darkness fast closing around them, would but make the route more difficult and dangerous.

Wearily and with fast increasing weakness the noble horse struggled on.   One satisfaction though he had, if his own horse was failing, so were those of his pursuers as well.   It was but a question of endurance, though it seemed almost decided against him, for his pursuers were gaining now.

"By gum," he muttered, "if my horse should stumble and fall."

And a shudder passed over him as he saw, in his imagination, the triumphant savages rush upon him.

(74)

A RACE FOR LIFE.

But a far more pleasing sight, just then, was revealed; for, on turning a bend in his course, he beheld the lights of the settlement scarcely a half mile away.

With a shout of joy, he raised in his saddle and looked back at his pursuers. One by one they had dropped out of the race, till but a half dozen of them remained.

Quick as thought Charley sprang from the saddle and discharged his Winchester at the formost. In the darkness, his aim was uncertain, but his object was understood, for hardly had the report broken the stillness, when the Indians dismounted and began a fusilade upon him. Charley kept up his firing, more to signal help than in the hope of hitting any of his foes.

But soon all trace of them was lost, for they did not care, even iu the darkness, to make target of themselves for him to practice upon. But Charley understood well enough that they would not yet give up the hope of killing him.

Maddened by the death of their comrades, and piqued at not being able to capture him, the savages threw themselves in the tall grass and began crawling toward him.

Charley saw their game, and to avoid them, began crawling away toward a stream a few yards distant. Here, sheltered by the trees and darkness, he waited and watched.

Presently, from down the valley toward the settlement, the unmistakable sound cf horses' hoofs upon the hard ground was heard. Had they heard his signal? Then a new thought struck him.

"By thunder now," he said, "if I can drown the sound

of those fellows till they get most here, we'll get some of these red devils yet!"

And in order to accomplish his object, he began firing, changing his position each time.

But the wily savages had either heard the approaching horsemen, or understood the ruse, for a few minutes later, when some ten or a dozen horsemen came dashing up, no trace of the Indians could be found.

Returning in a short time from the search, they all returned to the settlement.

————:0:————

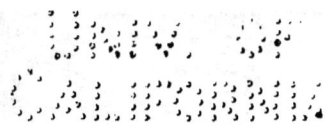

THE MURDERER HUNG.

CHAPTER XIII.

THE HAUNTED CABIN.

Not long after reaching the settlement, Charley heard the story of a foul and cowardly murder that had been committed some eight months before. All efforts to discover the murderer, had failed to bring to light even a small clew as to who the murderer was. Nor, even, conld the body be found.

"How do you know he was murdered then?" asked Charley.

"Well, stranger," said a miner, "thar be things that one knows an' yet can't tell jest how he knows it. But I'll tell ye the story an' then ye can jedge fer yourself.

"Old Dad Payne an' his girl an' boy came here last spring and began work in ther mines. There was a young feller came with them, an' he went to prospecting up in the gulch, some ten miles above here, whar he lived mostly alone. This feller was in love with old Dad's gal an' they war gon' to marry in the fall. All to onct this here feller disappeared an' thet's the last of him—no, not the last, fer his ghost still stays in the little cabin whar he lived."

"The cabin is haunted then, is it?" asked Charley skeptically.

"Thet's what yer call it."

"Where is this Dad Payne and his girl now?" queried Charley.

"They live out yonder." And he pointed out the cabin. "He'll tell yer all yer want ter know."

Calling upon Dad Payne, Charley mentioned the subject and said—

(77)

"Are you anxious to discover the murderer?"

"Yes," replied the old man quickly.

"Do you suspect any one here?"

"No," he replied.

"What could have been the motive for taking his life?"

"I know of none at all."

"Nor suspect anything?"

"Nothing at all."

"Well, said Charley, ready to go, "I shall look into the case a little, and, if I can make anything out of it, I will let you know as soon as possible."

"Thank you," said the old man. "You are welcome here at any time—call as often as you like."

"I shall be sure to avail myself of the privilege," replied Charley, and left.

In less than two days, Charley learned that a young man of the town was very much interested in the Payne family. He was a respectable young fellow, so everybody said, of moderate means and, it appeared, was well thought of by the Payne's.

Immediately a dislike sprang up between the two, just why, perhaps neither could tell. They met often at the Paynes', and not long after, a slight suspicion was aroused in the young detective's mind, that, perhaps, this young fellow might know something about the murder.

"Why is it," thought Charley, "that the fellow takes such a dislike to me? I never gave him the slightest cause. It's not jealousy, for I don't meddle with the girl. No, by thunder, it's something else—there's something back of all this!"

Charley soon found out that he was hindered in every way conceivable by this fellow; and it angered and all the more determined him to solve the mystery.

One warm, pleasant morning, about a week after his arrival at the settlement, he saddled his horse and, without letting any one know of his going, went up to the canon, where the haunted cabin of the murdered man was situated.

As he entered the deep, gloomy canon, a feeling of gloom and uneasiness stole over him. Try as he would to banish the thought of ghosts from his mind, they would come in spite of him.

Deeper and darker grew the canon, till, at last. he stood before the little cabin.

Dismounting, he entered the cabin and looked about. Everything was just as left by its owner. Bars, beds, clothing, camping and prospecting outfit—all undisturbed.

Sitting down upon a stool in front of the fire-place, he rested his chin in his hands and was soon lost in deep thought. How long he had sat thus, he knew not, when he was aroused by the frightened snorting of his horse. Springing to his feet, he rushed to the door, just in time to see his horse disappear down the canon.

What had frightened him was more than he could tell, but he determined to wait and watch.

For hours Charley paced back and forth, but as nothing appeared, he determined to follow his horse back home. So trudging down the canon, he made his way back.

Somehow, an uneasy feeling took possession of him, the flight of his horse troubled him. He was not afraid, fear was a stranger to him.

Suddenly, as if rising from the ground, the shadowy form of a man appeared directly before him and scarcely fifty yards distant. So sudden and unexpected was his appearance, that Charley could not tell, from what direction he had come.

The apparition walked, or rather it seemed, glided down the canon in the direction of the settlement.

Some strange, fascinating power seemed to lure rather then impel Charley to follow after. It seemed to him that he could not have done otherwise, had he tried.

Charley knew that he was following the ghost of the haunted cabin,

Suddenly, as he came to a narrow place in the canon and close under an overhanging cliff, the man stopped, threw up his hands and fell, but quickly sprang to his feet and dashed away down into the bottom of the deep canon, among the dense growth of bushes which grew there.

Impelled by some strange and irresistible force, Charley sprang forward and followed the fleeing phantom.

On forcing his way through the almost impenetrable thicket, and as he was nearly midway, he caught the gleam of some bright object lying in the grass, which a closer examination of proved to be a knife.

Picking up the knife, he forced his way through and came out on the other side and stopped and was examining the knife, when he was again startled by the appearance of a man, riding up the canon.

Crouching low behind the bushes, Charley watched. The horseman rode to the very spot where the strange scene had taken place, and dismounted. Leaving his horse, he began to search as if trying to find something.

"I must find it," he said to himself. "It is here some-where—it must be! It's the only evidence against me. Oh, if that d—d detective should find it! By heaven," he hissed, "I will put a bullet through his heart!"

Just then, he stopped and looked wildly about him— he had discovered Charley's tracks, and as the awful thought dawned upon his troubled mind, that perhaps he was already discovered, nearly drove him frantic.

After satisfying himself that no one was near, he began to search again.

Crawling upon his hands and knees, he made his way through the thicket and paused within a few feet of the tree behind which Charley was concealed.

"By the eternal!" he muttered, "I will go home and kill that damnable detective this very night. He will be at—"

"At where?" interrupted Charley.

With a terrible oath the guilty man sprang to his feet and faced his hated and now triumphant enemy.

"Curse you!" he cried, and in an instant the two men sprang together. But the murderer, though a powerful man, was no match for the dauntless, young giant; and in less than a second, he was hurled stunned and bleeding to the ground.

A few minutes later, bound hand and foot, he was left alone to endure the horrors of his guilty conscience till morning.

"Yes," said Charley, as he turned to go. "I will leave you to the tender mercies of the ghost of poor

Billy Jones. Ah, you and Billy were very good friends; no doubt he will pay you a visit by and by." Saying which Charley walked away and left him.

It was ten o'clock that night, when Charley reached the settlement. He went to the saloon where he knew that he would find a large crowd of the miners and town people gathered, and entering the room just in time to hear the remark—

"This here new-comer what yer calls Yankee Charley, he suspects Jim Stone as has a hand in the murder of Billy Jones."

"Where's Yankee Charley?" asked one. "I would like to hear what he's got to say about it, anyway."

"Here," said Charley, stepping forward and throwing the knife upon a billiard table, around which the people were standing. "I have just returned from the haunted cabin up there in Dead Man's canon. I found that knife there. See what you think of it."

For a few minutes not a word was spoken; then Payne picked up the knife and read the name on the handle—the name of Jim Stone.

Holding the knife above his head, so that every one could see it, he cried—

"Jim Stone is the murderer!"

"Where's Jim Stone?" cried a dozen voices in chorus.

"I will tell you where he is," cried Charley. "Not three hours ago I left him in Dead Man's canon; just across the gulch from the cliff below the cabin. He was hunting for this knife."

"To horse!" yelled Payne, "and bring him in."

"You will find him there; I left him bound hand and foot with the ghost of Billy Jones to keep him company," said Charley.

"We'll bring him, we'll bring him!" yelled a dozen. "Don't wait, he might escape!"

Twenty minutes later a half dozen men rode away to bring the doomed man, while others paraded the streets and kept the people awake.

Early the next morning the prisoner was led forth. No judge or jury was needed. There was no question as to his guilt. And even before he was brought forth, the rope was ready for his neck.

The knife was shown him and he was asked, what he had to say for himself. He refused to say anything about the matter; and then for the first time the people saw that he had lost his reason.

Thinking, perhaps, that he was trying to play crazy, in the hope of escaping his miserable doom by such a ruse, the rope was adjusted about his neck, and again he was asked what he had to say.

"Ha, ha," laughed the maniac. "And so you've come, have you?" And again rang out that wild laugh. "Oh, curse you, Billy Jones, curse you, I say!"

"Up with him!" cried a dozen voices. And in a moment he was dangling from a limb of a tree.

All the next day his body hung upon the limb, a lesson, as one old fellow said, to evil-doers.

"We allers leaves 'em hang fer a while," said another, "as a sort of warning to others of a like sort."

The next day a posse of men went to Dead Man's canon and found the grave of the murdered man beneath the tree where the murderer was captured. A pile of stones was erected to mark the spot and for a protection against the intrusion of animals.

The phantom was never seen after the death of the murderer.

———:o:———

THE CAVE OF DEATH.

CHAPTER XIV.

THE CAVE OF DEATH.

About three weeks after first arriving at the settlement, Charley, believing, from what he had seen and learned from the unfortunate Jack, while at Devil's canon, that there was gold there and, ambitious to solve the mystery of that strange place, if possible, and he believed it to be, for he was satisfied in his own mind, that there was nothing unnatural or unfathomable about the place, resolved to return to Devil's canon.

He did not believe in ghosts, in spite of what he had seen at Dead Man's canon; but the people, who accompanied him, did.

"But," they said, "ghosts or no ghost, if there's gold there we'll find it."

They had heard the wild, fanciful stories of the place, of its fabulous wealth of gold, and its strange and weird mystery; and when they learned, that Charley had been there, they were wild to get him to lead them to the mysterious land.

Such is the cupidity of man that he will brave any danger in the hope and effort of becoming rich. Though Charley knew that the danger was great, he believed that all, or nearley all, danger could be avoided. The cause, which he believed to be a natural one, of that mysterious influence, which had lured the unfortunate victims of the Devil't canon to their doom, could be found and avoided.

Thus, full of hope, they started out on their perilous expedition, arriving the next evening at the old camping place, where Charley and old Jack had first stopped.

Early the next morning they all started out for the strange canon and, shortly after, they passed through the deep, narrow defile and entered the land of death.

"Here," said Charley, "is the very spot where I saw, for the last time, the three men, whom I and my pard had shown to their last resting place."

A shudder passed over him, as he looked around upon the scene of death and desolation. Not a living thing within the bounds of those faded walls.

As he stood there, a queer feeling came over him—a feeling of indifference of what might happen—a feeling as of confusion, which almost robbed him of his self-possession. His brain was in a whirl. Visions of wealth and happiness lured him on.

A little to the right was an entrance to a cavern. It was the "Cave of Death", but to him, it seemed to offer naught but wealth and happiness.

Here, he realized, was the danger—here lay the mystery surrounding this strange and fatal land. This mysterious influence, which had so nearly overpowered him—which lured him on—but the cause he could not understand.

Realizing that in this mysterious influence was their great and, perhaps, only danger, he strove, with all his might, to overcome it and to retain his senses. But, at times, it seemed impossible for him to govern his own actions, but when he saw that his companions were laboring under the same influence, he redoubled his efforts.

Already his companions began to move on toward the cave, drawn on by that almost irresistible and mysterious power.

As they approached the cave the sound of noises, of laughter, of shrieks, and groans, fell upon their ears. It was, so 'tis said by the Indians, "the cries and groans of the tortured souls, of its fated victims."

Entering the cave, they stood in the gloaming of that mysterions light which illuminates the cave—a light, so tradition says, is reflected from rubies and diamonds—a light, supposed to possess the peculiar and fascinating power to blind the eyes of the doomed beholder.

It was a beautiful sight indeed which presented itself to their view. Huge pillars oi glittering quartz and glisteniug stalactites, reflecting their rainbow tints so dazzlingly bright and beautiful.

As their wondering eyes fell upon this fascinating scene, robbing them for a moment of all thought of danger, from afar down the cavern came a whistling, hissing sound, that the exited imagination of the men interpreted according as their imagination led them. One heard it as a despairing wail, another the shrieks of demons.

The men were completely fascinated. Such wild and uncanny stories had they heard of this strange place, that they were prepared to see and hear anything. Their imaginations were worked up to that point, that the stories which they had heard, took on a form to suit each individual fancy—thus no two saw nor heard the same things.

There was one thing that Charley had seen, and that was the careless indifference to the real danger before them, whatever that danger might be. Charley had nearly succumbed to the same fascinating power, but he

had, by sheer force of will, banished it; and now, as he
saw the condition of his companions, he realized why it
was that many, who were known to have gone there,
never returned.   Robbed of their senses, they had gone
and never to return.

Seeing their danger, Charley determined to rouse them
to their senses.   To accomplish which he stepped before
them and discharged his gun over their heads and cried
out—

"See here, boys, this won't do; there's danger here;
'rouse up and look sharp, for, we must explore this cave
if we expect to find anything here! Be careful now, and
look where you are going!"

Just then an awful cry, followed by the most hideous
and unearthly laughter rang through the cave.

"Great God!" cried some one, "what was that?"

"Ha–ha–h–a" came back the demon laugh.

"Boys!" said Charley, "I have heard that laugh before; it's the Crazy Hermit!"

Just then a cry from one of Charley's companions
startled him; and turning to see what was the matter,
he saw the unfortunate man just as he disappeared
through the broken floor of the cave.   This revealed the
true danger of the cave.   It banished the thought of
demons and devils in an instant.   It was quicksand. His
companions sprang forward, but it was too late; for,
poor fellow, he was gone.   The sacrifice of his life had
solved the mystery of that awful place.

Now, for the first time, they realized the danger that
they were in.   There was but a thin crust of lime and
sand forming the floor of the cave; and it was liable to

break at any moment. Like a sheet of thin ice, it looked safe, but the danger was only too plainly revealed by the sad fate of poor Jones.

Sadly and cautiously they turned and picked their way back toward the entrance. Their retreat was followed by that same hideous laugh that they had heard before.

As they emerged from the cave, they saw, what they had not seen before, the skulls and bones of hundreds of human beings scattered about upon the white, glittering sand—the victims of the Devil's canon—Indian prisoners and criminals, who had been compelled to enter this ''Vale of Death", condemned to die by the strange and mysterious power which lurked about the place.

Again, as soon as they emerged from the cave, that strong feeling which had come over them when they first entered the canon, came over them. This time, nearly overpowering them, for they had stopped longer and, consequently, were more exposed to the influence which caused it.

This peculiar feeling was caused by a poisonous gas arising from the ground, a gas similar to, or perhaps the same, as that found in some wells and old mines. This was the mysterious power—a power attributed to evil spirits by the Indians and the superstitious hunters— that first dulled the senses, robbing one of a sense of his danger and then, by a sort of intoxicating feeling, led the victim to his doom.

Realiziug their danger now, they started for the entrance of the canon as fast as they could; but so long had they been exposed, that it was with the greatest difficulty that they could move at all.

A cry from one of the men arrested them and, turning to see what was the matter, they saw him sink to the ground in a state of unconsciousness. Springing quickly to his assistance, the others dragged him to the entrance where a breath of fresh air soon revived them, though it was several hours before the unconscious man was able to walk.

————:o:————

THE DEATH OF THE CRAZY HERMIT.

CHAPTER XV.

A MYSTERY.

"Boys," said Charley, as they returned to camp, "I don't believe there's any gold nor diamonds in Devil's canon; nor could we get it if there was. I didn't see any sign of gold there. But I will tell you what I did find, or rather, what I heard there, and that is this—I heard the demon-laugh of the "Crazy Hermit", or the "Old Man of the Mountains", as he is called. Now, I have seen that fellow, and I know where he lives. It's over on the other side of the mountain. He lives in a cave over there and I think, that that cave and this one here are connected. I know that it was the Hermit that uttered that horrible laugh in the cave—I've heard it before.

"Now, I propose, that we go over there to-night. It will take us about three or four hours to make it. That will be just about the right time to see the ghost dance. What do you say?"

"We say, let's go!" exclaimed all. And in a few minutes they were making their way towards the gorge where Charley had witnessed the strange dance of the shadowy figures upon the cliff wall—the place where the Crazy Hermit had appeared and frightened away the savages.

Reaching the gorge, they followed the little brook to where it emerged from the thicket; here they camped.

"Do you see that black hole up there?" asked Charley.

"Well," he said, "the Hermit lives there, and he's got a

magic lantern or something up there and he will give us a free show pretty soon, I think; so watch."

They had not long to wait. It was about ten o'clock and everything was still. Suddenly upon the opposite wall appeared those shadowy figures, and, as if in accompaniment to the ghostly dance, that same hideous, demoniacal laughter, followed by and mingled with the most unearthly shrieks and cries that mortal ears ever heard.

Upon the opposite wall flitted and danced those shadowy figures. But, suddenly, a change came over the scene; a giant form appeared among them and, with a huge club, began felling the shadowy imps to the ground; no sooner did one fall than another arose and entered the never-ceasing combat.

Demon's or devil's, indeed, must have been the arm that wielded that huge club, for, hour after hour waged that fierce and never-to-be-forgotten conflict.

At last, as if by the interposition of some out-side cause, the fierce conflict ended, and again all was darkness and gloom.

"By ginger!" exclaimed Charley, "they gave us a little variation to the program to-night. I wonder, what it means, anyway?"

"What the dickens does he do that for, anyway?" queried one of the boys. "What's the meaning of it?"

"And how does he do it?" asked another.

"He's in league with the devil!" declared another

"Devil or no devil," said Charley, "we'll investigate the cave in the morning and solve the mystery."

And thus determined, they retired for the night.

In the morning, bright and early, they began searching for a means of reaching the cave above.

"I'll tell you, boys, said Charley, "I saw the Hermit
here, and I know, that he has some way to reach the
cave. If he can get there, we can, if we can only find
the way. Now, you can see that he always follows this
little brook through the thicket — the brook comes right
out from under the cliff and, I think, that it's the entrance to the cave."

By this time they had reached the cliff wall, from
under which came the little brook.

"There," said Charley, pointing to the place, "is the
entrance to the cave."

And taking a lasso which he carried, he fastened one
end of it around his waist and handing the other to the
boys, he continued—

"You fellows hold the rope, and I'll see what's in
there."

And taking a long breath, he ducked his head below
the water and crept forward. Feeling his way along, he
soon found, that he could ralse his head above water.

"By jingoes!" he exclaimed, as he raised his head
above the water and looked around. "I thought so!"
And jerking on the line to attract the attention of those
outside, he shouted to them to come in.

A few minutes later, all were in and ready to explore
the cave.

Following a narrow passage that gradually ascended
to a higher level, they soon came out into a large
room. Upon the sandy floor of this room the bare-
foot tracks were found. An opening in the side of

this room led out of the cliff wall and let the light of day shine in so that it was tolerably well lighted.

,,This must be the place," said Charley, ''where the old Hermit performs his tableaux. But where's he?"

Yes," said one of the men, going to the opening, "this is the place, I can see our camp below."

It was from this room that those awful cries had come; and it was in this room, that that terrible conflict was waged. But where was the giant of the contest of the night before?

An exclamation of one of the men drew the attention of all to another room, directly opposite the opening in the cliff; and, hurrying in, they found the dead body of the Hermit lying in the centre of the room. By his side lay the huge, knotted club, and grasped in one hand was the great nugget, for which he had commited the awful crime that made him a maniac, a demon.

Lying there, where he had fallen from sheer exhaustion, never to rise again, lay the Crazy Hermit. but where were the strange imps or whatever it was, that had caused the shadowy figures upon the cliff wall the night before? With what was he engaged?

''By thunder, I believe he was engaged last night with the devil himself," said Charley. ''If he was not, with what was he engaged?"

''Reader, we leave you this mystery to solve, we could not do it," declared Charley.

For two weeks they camped there and explored the cave daily, yet, when they left, they knew as little about the mysterious happenings, as when they first came. One thing they had learned—there was no gold there, except the huge nugget they had found in the dead Hermit's hand.

"Well," said Charley, as they were ready to leave, "we have got enough to pay us for our trouble anyway, so let the mystery rest for some one else to fathom, but I doubt, whether it will ever be done; for with the death of the Hermit ends the mission of those ghostly shadows which were reflected by that pale, weird light upon the face of the cliff.

Thus, after two weeks fruitless search for the fabulous wealth for gold and diamonds, which were reported to exist there, they gave up the search and returned to the settlement.

"Now I am ready for another trip somewhere," said Charley. "By gum, I can't lay around here more than one day. I must put in my time well, for there's no telling when I will get a chance to take another summer's vacation! By jinks, though, but I have had a ripping time so far anyhow! Only been out a little over two months either; Lord, but won't I have lots of fun yet, though! Ka-hoop! O Lord!"

———:o:———

CHAPTER XVI.

The next day, after returning to the settlement, Charley was overjoyed at meeting with a prospecting expedition that was going into the mountains away to the south-west. It was in these mountains, so old Jack had told him, that an old hermit had lived for many years. The country was almost unknown at that time.

A journey of five days brought them to the mountains.

One day, as they were passing along a small stream, they came out into a beautiful little park. Surrounded on all sides, as it was, by dense forests, from whose dark, somber shades rose the rugged, snow-capped mountains, and iu the centre of which nestled a beautiful little lake, it did indeed make a most pleasing picture. As they had reached the part of the country for which they set out, they concluded to make their camp there.

As Charley was no prospector, he assumed the duty of supplying the camp with wild game.

For several days he hunted about the forests and hills, bringing in a bountiful supply of venison and bear meat.

Often, in his rambles along the streams, he busied himself in prospecting on his own account, though he was nut successful. But one day, about a week after his arrival there, he was walking along a little stream, when he came upon the skeleton of a man. He had lain undisturbed and had undoubtedly been murdered, for, on examining the remains, Charley found a knife stick-

An Unfinished Letter.

ing between the ribs, directly over the region of the heart.

In a pocket of his partially decayed coat, Charley found a letter, which disclosed the secret of the disapearance of twelve young men.

The letter read thus—

—"Twelve days ago we started on our flight. Pursued by the Indians, we fled away into the mountains and forests, not knowing where we were agoing. We had pro—" Here a part of the letter was so soiled and discolored, that it was impossible to make it out—"an awful death—a death so mysterious and sad—. At exactly sunset each day one of us must die. Oh God! the horror that fills my heart at the thought of that awful, mysterious and fatal power that has robbed my eleven companions of life.

"Oh God! I feel, even now, the icy hand of death closing upon my heart; for the hour has almost come, when I, the last of the twelve, must also die, as my companions have died. Yes, the bright, beautiful sun, upon which I can never look again, is fast going down behind the western mountains; and with its setting must I die. Oh God! upon this the twelfth day, I alone am the victim; for I, alone, of the twelve brave boys, am left.

"But yesterday, there were two of us, as the sun went down, we looked in each others faces, and I saw the unmistakable sign that my companion and not I would be the victim of that hour. He asked me to get him a cup of water, complaining that he felt sick. I hurried to the brook and got the water and returned, to find, alas!

what I expected, the dead body of my companion.   He had fallen pierced to the heart by his own dagger.

"Crazed and horrified by the awful fate of my companions, I wandered away into the forests, not knowing nor caring where I was going; for I knew that my fate was inevitable—I could live but another day. And now, as the sun—the last of my life—is slowly sinking in the west, I feel the coming of the Destroyer—the Avenger.

"I look back to the past—I see my friends again at home, and I know that they will never solve the mystery of my death, for I, the last of the twelve, have not witnessed the death of one. It always happened that they were stricken down when no one was looking. Fate had decreed it thus.

"I will fold this letter and put it in my pocket-book, so, if chance should happen to guide some wandering eye to my lonely remains, it may be found, and, perhaps, convey a poor and very limited idea of the suffering and, at last, the death of the last of the twelve, and here will I await my doom."

After reading the letter, Charley placed it in his pocket and, gathering up what articles there were that were of any use or that might serve as a clew to the identity of the unfortunate man, he returned to camp.

That evening, after supper, as they were all sitting around smoking, he told of the adventure of the day and read them the letter. No one had ever heard of such a party.

Shortly after this, as Charley was out hunting, he came upon the tracks of a bear. He concluded to trail him and, if possible, to capture him.

Following the trail down a deep canon, he came suddenly upon an old man, as he was sitting upon a fallen tree. His head, white as the driven snow, was bowed low and he seemed to be lost in deep thought. He arose quickly, as Charley came up, and stood leaning on his gun, watching his visitor closely.

He was a man of some fifty years. As Charley came up, he said—

"How do you do, stranger?"

Charley returned the greeting and said—

"I did not expect to meet anyone here."

"Nor I," replied the old man; "you are the first man I have seen for more than a year."

"Rather a lonely life you are leading, I should say," declared Charley.

"Lonely!" exclaimed the old man in a sad, melancholly tone. "Yes, I am lonely—all alone and doomed to eternal disappointment. "O God," he moaned "that I could but find a trace of him; I could die in peace!"

"You seem to be in trouble," said Charley. Can't I do anything for you?"

"I don't know," he mused, and looked away over the mountain peaks, with a dull, meaningless expression in his sad, gray eyes.

"I don't know," he reiterated, "but come to my cabin, I want to talk a little with you."

And he led the way in silence, till they reached his cabin.

"Here," he said, "is where I have lived for three years; come in."

It was a neat, comfortable little place. Charley sat
down upon a pile of furs, while the old man busied himself preparing supper.

After supper, they seated themselves before the fire,
and for a long time the old man was lost in deep thought;
his head bowed and gazing intently into the fire. Finally arousing himself, he said—

"I believe that my dream is coming true. I dreamed
the other night that my mission was ended—that a
stranger came to my cabin, bringing to me the news
that my long lost boy's remains had been found."

"Tell me the story," said Charley, "and perhaps I
can help you. I will gladly do anything that I can for
you."

"Ten years ago," he said, "I was a prosperous
merchant in San Francisco. I had a son, an only child,
of twenty years of age, bright, noble fellow.

Here the tears coursed down the old man's cheeks and
his frame shook with the emotion he could not sup-
press.

"He was ambitious," continued the old man, "to do
some great thing—to accomplish some great undertak-
ing. I knew his ambitious aspirations, and I knew the
uselessness of trying to dissuade him—I remembered
when I was a boy like him, the ambitious feelings that
filled my heart, when I left home and set out to seek
my fortune in the mines of California.

"About this time a wild and, to me, incredible story,
of a great diamond that had been discovered among a
tribe of Indians, living in the eastern part of Idaho,
reached the city. The story, as told by an old miner,

created considerable excitement. It was called the 'Great Medicine-stone', and was by the Indians considered invaluable. It was guarded night and day by twelve chosen warriors.

"This was the heighth of my boy's ambition—to go there and possess himself of that stone. So he and his associates, twelve altogether, started for the Indian country.

"For two months he kept me posted about his journey. Every few days I would receive a letter, setting forth, even to the minutest details, all the happenings of his journey. As they neared the land of the Idahoes, stories of the wonderful 'Medicine-stone' convinced them of its existence, and of the difficulty they would encounter in getting it. The last letter was written as they were encamped about two miles from the Indian village.

"Days and months passed, still no tidings came. His poor mother, broken-hearted, sank day by day under the weight of that awful fear which weighed down her heart, to an untimely grave.

"An insatiable desire to solve the mystery of my son's fate possessed me, and so I set out for the Indian country. On arriving at the Indian village, I found the remnants of a once powerful and intelligent tribe, dwindled away almost to nothing.

"From an old half-breed, with whom I stopped, I learned this story: 'Over one hundred years ago, an old medicine man of the tribe had seen in a vision, a great diamond lying in a great river far to the north-west. In his vision he was told, that he who possessed this wonderful stone would live forever, provided he always kept it and used it for the good of his people; but to others than those of pure heart and unselfish motives, it would bring ruin and misfortune. It would protect him and his people against their enemies, against disease, and in its liquid depths he could read the future destiny of any-one who looked upon it. The old medicine man had made the journey, encountering many hardships and dangers, but had, at last, brought the stone in triumph to his tribe, with whom it had remained for over a hundred years. A great many attempts by their enemies had been made to obtain the wonderful stone. Once a powerful tribe, who live far to the south, some three thousand strong, attacked their village. But the Great Medicine-man appeared in the midst of the battle, bearing the 'Great Medicine-stone' aloof, so that it shot its glimmering rays upon the enemy. Instantly the enemy fell down and perished. Three thousand warriors perished and their bodies were taken to a cave close by, where their bones remain to this day. This cave is called the 'Cave of Bones'.

"But a short time ago," said the half breed, "the old medicine-man called the tribe together and told them of a vision of coming misfortune which he had seen. The vision was not clear, yet he knew that they would lose the 'Great Medicine-stone'. They were to come from a large city on the shore of the great water to the West. They would gain possession of the 'Stone' and then flee away to the mountains. All attempts to regain the 'Stone', would be in vain, but the robbers would never return to their homes; for the avenging spirit of the old medicine-man would pursue them, and, one by one, each day at exactly the time when the 'Stone' was stolen, one of the thieves would fall, pierced through the heart with his own knife and with his own hand."

The old man's voice trembled with emotion as he related the strange story, and for some time, after he was done speaking, he sat in silence, lost in thought.

"For six days," he continued, "the Indians pursued the fugitives, and each day finding the lonely grave of one of them. On the eleventh day a great storm arose and blotted out the trail, so that they could not follow any farther.

"I hired the half breed to guide me to the graves. Strange to say the bodies had not been disturbed, and I easily recognized them by various articles; but the remains of my boy were not found. Then commenced the long and tedious search. For two months I searched in every direction, when I found another grave. Nearly two years passed before I found the eighth grave. Two months later, I found the ninth. Two years more, and I found the tenth, and three years after, I found the eleventh, but none of them contained the remains of my son. He was spared to the last, that he might suffer the greater torment."

Here the old man's voice failed, and, burying his face in his hand, he burst into tears.

"I could well understand the awful suffering which had racked the old man's brain till he was bereft of his reason," said Charley in relating the story, "for he was indeed a maniac."

"Oh God!" cried the old man, "that I could find the remains of my boy, I could then die in peace; it's my last wish—my only prayer."

"Old man," said Charley, laying his hand upon the bowed head, ''perhaps I can help you in this. Read this letter," and Charley handed him the letter which he had found.

Eagerly he grasped the letter from Charley's hand and scanned its contents closely. Charley could see that a terrible struggle was waging within him. His hand shook and the hot tears blinded his eyes.

"Oh God," he cried, "at last, at last, my prayer is answered; but another day and I am ready to die!"

Charley lay down upon a bed in the corner, aud went to sleep; but when morning came, he knew, that the old man had not slept. He sat where he was when Charley left him the evening before.

Soon after breakfast, Charley led the old man to where the remains of his long lost son lay. He recognized the things as those belonging to his boy.

For several moments he stood speechless, yet calm, then his head drooped upon his bosom and he tottered. Charley sprang forward and caught him, and then laid him gently down upon the ground. a corpse.

That night, while sitting around the fire, Charley told the story of the old man and his wanderings.

The legend of the 'Great Medicine-stone' was known by the miners. Their story of it was the same, as that told by the old man. They described it as a very large diamond, perfectly transparent, and having twelve equal faces—as if cut and polished in the most perfect manner. But whether cut by art or nature, no man could tell.

"Where can this great diamond be?" was asked by all. "Had the old man found it? Would he be apt to take it if he had, knowing its history and the awful suffering it brought upon those who possessed it? If he had found it, what had he done with it?"

"No," said Charley, "I don't believe that he found it. If he had, he would have said something about it."

They determined to search the cabin at any rate; so the next morning they went and, after burying father and son in one grave, went to the cabin.

When they came near, they saw a column of smoke rising from the valley near the cabin; and, soon after, saw a band of Indians riding away.

On reaching the cabin, they found, that it had been robbed of everything worth carrying away.

On the floor was a diary relating the details of the old man's long and tedious search. Upon one page was an account of his finding the 'Great Medicine-stone'; and upon the last page, and written the night that Charley had stayed with him, were the words—

"Knowing that you will return to my cabin, and desiring to pay you for the kindness you have shown me, I bequeath you all my property. Raise the large stone in front of the fire-place, and there, you will find the 'Great Medicine-stone' of the Idahoes, also a few nuggets of gold that I picked up in my wanderings."

But other eyes had read that page, and other hands had raised that stone, and borne away the treasure.

—————:o:—————

CHAPTER XVII.

With a feeling of disappointment at the loss of fortune so nearly won, yet so hopelessly lost, they turned from the cabin and went back to camp.

Here another disappointment was in store for them; for, in their absence, the Indians had raided their camp, completely destroying everything which they did not carry away.

"Boys," said Charley, "we'd better get out of here before those devils take it into their heads to come back again and take us in. I've got all the prospecting I want, for a while at least, so, I think, that I will look for something else."

"What will you try?" asked one.

"Oh, I don't know," replied Charley.

"Let's follow up the trail of that diamond," said another.

"Let's go back to the settlement," suggested a third.

So, after a little further discussion, it was decided best to return to the settlement.

The nearest settlement was some thirty miles to the west of them, and to this settlement they went.

Two days after reaching the town, which was called 'Hardscrabble', Charley stepped into a place called 'The Eldorado'. It was a dance hall and gambling den—a low, disreputable place.

Two long, dreary, monotonous days had passed, without an event of any kind having happened to cheer up the flagging spirits of our young tourist.

(106)

CHARLEY AND FRANK SMITH.

"By jinks," exclaimed Charley, "this won't do; my summer's vacation must not be spoiled; something must be did right away! By gum, if something don't turn up by another day, I'm off just a-flying."

Scarcely two hours after this the town of Hardscrabble was thrown into a state of feverish excitement by the report that a man—a stranger—had been shot while passing along the street.

Now, if it had been a citizen, no one would have taken any particular notice of it; for such incidents are of frequent occurence.   But when a stranger falls, and that, too, by the hand of an unknown assassin, in the midst of the hospitable town of Hardscrabble, "thar'll be suthin' did!"

The one thing above all else that Hardscrabble boasts of, is her hospitality toward strangers.   Here an unpardonable offence had been committed and the people were bent on vengeance.

Rough, but kind hands, raised the stranger and bore him to the nearest house.   It happened to be the house where Charley was staying, and he was one of the first to go to the fallen stranger's assistance.   Here, for a week, he lay first upon this side and then upon that of that dark and mysterious line which separates this life from the life eternal.

At last the crisis came.   The attentive watcher, who had watched and cared for him so tenderly, saw that the critical moment had arrived.

Slowly the stranger's eyes opened and, for a moment, rested upon the face of the watcher;   then turning away he murmured—

"Ah, yes, it was all a dream! But oh, what makes me feel so weak and faint? Where am I?" he asked, turning an inquiring look upon his nurse. "What has happened? Where is she? Zell, Zell! Oh, where is she?"

"Hush," said Charley, kindly; "you are too weak to talk much; you have been shot, and you must keep quiet for a lit—"

"Oh my God!" he moaned, "then it is not all a dream —I have seen her, I have seen Zell!"

"You must keep quiet," cautioned Charley; "you must not take on so; your life may depend upon it—do you understand?"

"Yes, yes; but how long have I been here?" he asked anxiously.

"Six days," answered Charley.

"Six days! Is it possible that I have been here so long?"

"It was just six days ago to-day that I had you brought here."

"And have you been here with me all that time?" he asked.

"Nearly all the time."

"Have I talked much?" he queried in a troubled, anxious tone.

"Yes, you have talked a good deal."

For a few minutes he was silent, then he asked, anxiously —

"Has any one beside you heard much that I have said?"

"No," answered Charley, "not, but a very little."

A sigh of relief was his only answer.

A few days later, as Charley came into his room, the invalid asked—

"Are you much acquainted with the country around here?"

"No," answered Charley, "I have only been here for a short time and am not much acquainted, neither with the country nor the people."

"There's a man somewhere in this part of the country that is living the life of a hermit. He lives here somewhere in the mountains and he has his daughter with him. Possibly you may have heard of him?"

"I don't know," answered Charley; "I have heard of several hermits; possibly I may have heard of this one," answered Charley, immediately interested. "Do you think that he lives near here?"

"Yes, I think that he does. I have a good reason for thinking so."

"I have heard," said Charley, "that there's an old man living in the mountains somewhere out here in the country. But who is the hermit that you speak of? Is he a friend of yours?"

"Yes, he is a friend," answered the invalid, "and I am very anxious to find him."

"Perhaps that I can aid you. Tell me what you know of his whereabouts, and I will see what I can do."

"It is a long story," he said, "a story that I would not tell to other than a friend. You have been a friend to me and I believe, that I can trust you. This hermit's name is James Barnes. A few years ago, he was a rich and prosperous merchant in New York. He still has a son and married daughter living there. He

has another daughter, his youngest, with him, wherever
he is.   This daughter, Zell, is about seventeen now.
She had a lover," he resumed after a short pause, ''and
for a time, all went well.   But there came a change.
Mr. Barnes was unfortunate in his business transactions,
and, as is too often the case, through the treachery of
supposed friends, he was ruined.   The great misfortune
that has befallen him, together with some business
affair that he was unable to clear up, drove him from
his home and friends to this country, where he has
buried himself and daughter in obscurity."

   "If I mistake not, you are, or ought to be the girl's
lover," said Charley."

   "Yes," he answered, ''I loved her, ''but there was
another, a more fortunate woer than I; for he was rich
and I but a poor clerk in her father's store.   Still the
girl gave encouragement,   while her father forbade me
to see her and, at the same time, urged her to accept
my rival.   There was some business transaction that
my rival knew of, that implicated Mr. Barnes crimin-
ally.   My rival used his knowledge of this affair to
further his suit;   and Mr. Barnes, in order to save himself, urged Zell to accept him.   But she refused.   To
escape punishment, Mr, Barnes was compelled to leave
No one knew where he went;   but I have traced him to
this country and since I came here I have learned something which convinces me that he is here   I saw Zell
the night I was shot.   I saw her in company with my
old rival, Jim Kingsbury."

   "Do you know what the secret is which this Kingsbury threatened to expose?" asked Charley.

"No," he replied, "I don't know."

"Well I can enlighten you a little on this matter; I am a detective and I have worked a little on this case. These parties—for Miss Barnes is implicated in this matter as well as her father—are forgers. Miss Barnes is an expert penman and was, no doubt, induced to do the work which her father was unable to do."

"Sir," said the invalid indignantly, "don't tell me that Zell is a forger!"

"Yes, she is a forger, and there's a reward of ten thousand dollars offered for their arrest and return to New York."

"I don't believe it!" he said, "you are misinformed, about her, at least."

"Not hardly, my friend; but I want to ask you a few questions now. First—what is your name?"

"My name is Frank Smith."

"Do you know who it was that shot you?" asked Charley.

"Yes. It was Jim Kingsbury."

"He wished to get you out of the way, I suppose. Do you think that he knows where this Mr. Barnes lives?"

"Yes, he must; for I saw Zell with him."

"I will look this girl up. Do you know where she is, or was, staying when you saw her?"

"No, I saw them down town."

"And she was with Kingsbury."

"Yes."

"Well, I will look him up too."

CHAPTER XVIII.

KITTY.

Straying along the street that evening, Charley came to the Eldorado. Entering the large and already well filled hall, he seated himself and was watching the gay throng of dancers; but no sign of Kingsbury was to be seen. After satisfying himself that he was not there, the young detective arose to go, when he was accosted by a tall, handsome fellow, known as the "Masher."

"Hello, old fellow!" exclaimed the masher.

"All right, masher, how's yourself?" replied Charley.

"Just as you please, Charley," replied the masher gayly. "But say, old fellow, who is that pretty girl over there? See?" and he pointed her out.

"Don't know, masher; never saw her before," replied Charley, looking at the girl closely. Some gay siren, I suppose—which was not true, for Charley knew the girl only too well; for it was none other than his little friend Kitty Barnes, the very girl of all others that he would most like to see. "Ah, but she is a beauty though, isn't she?"

"She's a daisy!" he exclaimed, "a perfect beauty! honest, now, don't you know her?"

"Never saw her before," declared Charley emphatically.

"Don't believe it, Charley!" said the masher. "I saw her looking at you when you came in as though she knew you."

"Why don't you go and get acquainted with her? you are a masher—go in and try your luck."

CHARLEY AND KITTY.

"I'll wager a new hat that I dance with her the next set," he said.

"I never bet, but if I did, I would take you up."

"Ah, here's the masher!" cried a half dozen giddy girls, as they seized him and dragged him away, each one claiming him as her partner.

"And I claim this gentleman as my partner." said a tremulous, faltering voice; and a light hand was laid upon Charley's arm.

"Kitty, I did not expect to find you in such a place as this! What does it mean, Kitty, have you deceived me?" he asked in a tone of reproach.

"Oh Charley, don't speak to me that way, don't distrust me—I am all right; believe me, Charley, I am an honest girl, indeed I am!"

"I don't want to distrust you, Kitty, but I didn't expect to find you here. Well, how are you getting along anyway, Miss Kitty?"

"Oh, I am well of course—I am always well. But how have you prospered since I saw you last?"

"All right, Miss—"

"Don't 'Miss' me, please! It makes me tired!"

"All right," replied Charley, "henceforth, then, it's just plain Kitty."

"That will suit me. Do you dance?"

"No, I never dance."

"Nor drink, nor gamble, nor play cards. I can trust you, Charley."

"I hope, I am worthy of your confidence. Have you been dancing?"

"No. Oh, I just love to dance! Can't you dance? Honest now?"

"No, no, Kitty. Why didn't you dance with the masher; didn't he ask you?"

"Yes, but I don't care for such a partner—no, no, Charley, I don't want to dance here, I didn't come here to dance; though I would dance with you—you danced with me once, don't you remember, Charley?"

"I should say that I do! I won't forget that night very soon, I can tell you! But, Kitty, what are you doing here?"

"My brother John brought me here," she said.

"And where is he?"

"I don't know; we have quarreled—we couldn't get along, so he left me here."

"The miserable scoundrel—"

"Don't, Charley, please don't!" she exclaimed. "He is my brother."

"No brother would leave a sister in such a place as this!"

"Oh, he didn't leave me here in this house, Charley. I came here to see if I couldn't find him. I know what kind of a place it is, Charley, and I know the risk I run in coming here, but I have run risks before. But I want to tell you what has happened. I can trust you, I know. I am in trouble and I want a friend."

"You need not go any further, Kitty. We swore once that we would always be friends; and I repeat my vow now. So help me God, Kitty, I will honor you as I would my own sister; you need have no fear of me!"

"Thank you, Charley; and may God bless you for it! I will do whatever you advise me to do."

"Tell me what has happened."

"About a week ago, that detective that was with you,

down at Bozeman, came back from Cincinnati and raided our place. My brother Frank, uncle Dick and another man were captured and taken back to Cincinnati. Father was killed, and I and my brother John, made our escape and came here. My brother found an old acquaintance here; he was working some scheme and, of course, John went in with him. This is what made the trouble between John and I. He accused me of treachery. He would never trust me after I helped you to escape that night at Bozeman. So he left me."

"When did he leave you?"

"This morning," answered Kitty. He and Jim Kingsbury—"

"Jim Kingsbury! By thunder—"

"Please, don't swear, Charley! Do you know him?" asked Kitty.

"Yes. Do you know where he went?"

"No, not exactly. But I heard them talking last night about going south into the mountains. There's an old hermit that lives there whom they want to find," said Kitty.

"Do you know why they want to find him?"

"No, I don't," she said, "but Jimmy is very anxious to find him; but I couldn't find out what for. There was something said about a girl; and there was something said about a diamond—"

"You say that he lives south of here in the mountains?"

"That's what Jim said."

"And there was something said about a girl?"

"Yes. That interests you, don't it? But why are you

so interested, Charley; do you know anything about them? or is it the girl?"

"Hang the girls!" exclaimed he. "I have no faith in them—they are but a fickle set of nuisances!"

"Is that your opinion of me, sir?" asked Kitty quickly. "But never mind; I will show you!"

"No Kitty, I don't think that of you; you know I don't. But this hermit and his daughter—Yes I know them, or of them. I am searching for them; and I came here to-night in the hope of learning something about them. I was fortunate indeed, that I found you here."

"You will be almost tempted to forgive me for being here then, won't you?" she laughed.

"Almost; yes I will be altogether tempted and more too. But it is getting late and we must go home—"

"Go home!" she said sadly. "Oh, that I had a home to go to, a friend in whom I could confide!"

"Remember Kitty, I am your friend. Can't you trust me?" asked Charley.

"Yes, yes, I can trust you, Charley, but I don't ask you to burden yourself with me—a girl is a 'nuisance' you know."

"There's no need of your being a burden to anyone. If I had a dozen such pretty girls as you, I could find a dozen young fellows anxious and ready to relieve me of my burdens—pretty girls are always at a premium."

"Thank you Charley, thank you; you are very kind to me. I have some money and can pay my way all right; though I don't like to be alone."

"Come home with me; it's a good place and you will like it there. You will be in good company and well treated there. Do you want to go to your boarding place first, or will you go with me now?"

"I will go with you if you think that it will be all right."

Oh, it will be all right, never fear. The landlady is a kind old soul and will be only too glad to take you in. Be honest with her and don't try to deceive her about anything. 'Honesty is the best policy.'"

"So you have told me before; but I am not ashamed of my conduct, I don't want to deceive anyone," she said. "Though I have been found in bad company and am a counterfeiter's daughter, I am not dishonest."

"Easy now, don't get angry at me. I may talk rather plain some times, but I mean well by you, Kitty."

"Oh, I am not angry at you; I know your advice is good; I know that you mean well by me. Say whatever you please to me, Charley, it's all right."

"No more now, for here's my boarding house. Come in and I will introduce you to my hostess."

Entering the parlor, Charley introduced his little friend and consigned her to the care of the motherly old lady.

"Well, what news?" asked the invalid, as Charley entered his room. "Did you find the girl?"

"Good news," replied Charley, "and, yes I found the girl. I have found a clew which, I think, will guide me to the hermit's retreat; besides, I found the girl you saw, and brought her home with me."

"Where is she? let me see her!" he cried excitedly.

"Not to-night. It is not Zell at all. It is her cousin Kitty."

"Then it's not the girl I saw," he said in disappointment.

"Yes, it's the same girl; she was with Kingsbury."

"Let me see her!"

"Not to-night. I must be off directly. I am going down there and look up this Barnes," said Charley.

"When will you start?"

"In five minutes," said Charley. "I will leave my little friend Kitty with you."

"Your friend?"

"Yes, she is an old friend of mine."

"Won't you introduce her to me before you go?" he asked.

"No, I will leave that to the landlady. I will leave her with you to keep you company, and all I ask is that you don't lose your head or your heart as the case may be, before I return."

"Never fear, your friend will be safe with me. I suppose, she is a very particular friend, eh?"

"Oh no! just an every day friend, that's all. But I give you fair warning—she's dangerous. But I must be off. I don't want any one to know anything about it, so I will go to-night."

A half hour later he was on the way to the mountains which lay some thirty miles to the south, and by morning, had reached the foot hills.

————:o:————

A HEINOUS CRIME.

CHAPTER XIX.

THE PLOTTERS.

"Kingsbury," said John Barnes, "what is your plan? If I am to take a hand in this matter, I must know all about it. I want to know just what I am to get out of it; it's a job I don't exactly like. Old Barnes is an uncle of mine; but, of course, he must be put out of the way. He's getting old anyway and it won't shorten his lease of life but a little, at most. But how are we to operate? And what am I to get out of it? That's the point."

"I will give you a thousand dollars, or we will divide the plunder between us; just as you choose. The old man, so the Indians say, has considerable wealth. There's a half-breed that I got acquainted with, that told me of a diamond which the old man purchased from some Indians that is worth a fortune. There's a legend connected with the stone, which is reported by the Indians."

"But I have no faith in the stories of these Indians!" exclaimed Barnes. "He may have a diamond or he may have nothing at all. There's no confidence to be placed in the stories of these Indians."

"Well, I don't know about that," said Kingsbury, "I have heard of this diamond before. It is called the 'Great Medicine-stone', and according to the stories of white men that have seen it, it must be very valuable."

"Well, I will go and help you get the girl, and if we get the stone, I will take that for my share and you may have the girl—you said, she was all you wanted," said Barnes.

"Yes," said Kingsbury, "the girl is all I want."

"Well, how are we to operate?"

"I will tell you. We will go down to the Indian village and get a few of them to go with us. They know where the old man lives, and will help us for the plunder."

"But won't they give us trouble? If they know about this diamond, they will try to get it."

"A half dozen of them is all we want; we can manage that many all right. A couple quarts of whisky will put them in shape, so that we can dispose of them," he said; and there was a wicked gleam in his evil eyes, as he said it.

"Yes," said Barnes, "that plan will work all right; but how are we to dispose of the old man, so that the girl will know nothing about it?"

"Oh, that's just as easy—we must get the Indians to make an attack upon the cabin, kill the old man and capture the girl; then we will come in and rescue her, of course. That will make it appear all right."

"That's all right as far as the girl is concerned, but the stone, how are we to find that?"

"The girl will know all about it. If the old man has hid it, she will know where it is. But the chances are that she has it herself."

Thus, as the two men rode on toward the Indian village, they laid their plans. One to gain possession of a valuable diamond, the other to gain possession of a beautiful girl, and both, to not only rob an old man, but to murder him as well.

After reaching the village, they found no difficulty in obtaining the desired assistance. The half-breed, of whom Kingsbury had spoken, and five others, were hired for a small sum and the promise of plunder.

These Indians knew where the old hermit lived, and soon led the two white men to the vicinity. Here they camped to watch for an opportunity to carry out their villainous plot.

A week had passed, still, as yet, nothing had been done. The two white men, disguised as Indians, had visited the hermit, and had watched him day by day, in hopes of learning something about the treasure. But as yet, nothing had been learned.

"John," said Kingsbury, as he returned one day from a fruitless visit to the hermitage, "the old man has gone out hunting; I watched him till I was satisfied where he was going; Now I propose, that we follow him and settle this business with him, without the aid of the Indians. I believe that he carries the diamond with him. If he does, we can get it, and the Indians won't be none the wiser nor richer. Once the old man is out of the way, I can manage the girl all right."

This was agreed to; and so, taking their guns, the two men followed the hermit's trail for two or three miles, when they came suddenly upon him in a dark, dreary part of the forest.

He was standing with his back toward them and did not hear their stealthy approach.

"Ah," whispered Kingsbury, as he caught the gleam of some bright, glittering object which the hermit was holding in his hand? "it's the diamond! "Now," he whispered, "is our time!"

Instantly two rifles were raised, and then, almost at the instant of the report, the old man turned and saw the assassins; but it was too late. Two reports rang out upon the still evening air and the old hermit, uttering a cry of anguish, fell.

Wrestling the blood-bought treasury from the nerveless fingers, the assasins fled.

"Now," said Kingsbury, as they made their way back toward camp, "for the girl. The Indians shall make their attack to-night, and before morning, I will rescue Zell and bear her away in triumph!"

"Quite likely that you can manage the girl all right, but I want to tell you that, if she is anything like Kitty, you will have trouble with her!"

"Oh, I can manage her; never fear. She isn't like Kitty. She is as quiet and gentle as a lamb—"

"Yes, and so is Kitty. She is all right if any one uses her right; but you just stroke her the wrong way of the fur, and then look out!"

"Well, I will take my chances on that. All I ask, is to get her in my power, and I will guarantee, that before many days she will be willing to marry me. Yes, by the time that we reach the settlements, I will have her persuaded."

Thus this consumate villain, plotting the ruin of a fair young girl, whose hands were still red with the life-blood of her father, and in company with the girl's own cousin, boasted of his hellish plan in language that can not be used here.

————:o:————

CHARLEY AND ZELL.

CHAPTER XX.

ZELL.

It was a little after daylight when Charley reached the foothills and stopped to eat a bite which he had brought along with him. He had learned that there was an Indian village somewhere near, and he decided to look it up and try to learn something from them. This he did; for he was fortunate in finding the village that day along toward evening.

Here he learned that the old hermit lived about ten miles to the southwest. Setting out in that direction, he searched for several days without finding the hermitage.

One day, along toward evening, tired and almost starved, he was following along a little brook in the dark and al nost impenetrable forest, when he emerged into a small opening, almost in the centre of which stood a neat, little log cabin.

It was a pretty picture. Surrounded upon all sides as it was by snow-capped mountains and dark, evergreen forests. But beautiful as was the scene, his eyes rested upon an object that, in that wild, strange land, quickly banished all thoughts of nature's scenic beauty from his mind. This object was a girl. Graceful in form, beautiful in feature, she stood a veritable fairy queen. With large, lustrous, blue eyes and golden hair, which hung in one long braid far below her waist like a braid of shining gold. Arrayed in a neat, close fitting costume which showed her slight figure in graceful outlines, she made a picture that, in that wild, rough country, was well calculated to make glad the heart of a young man.

An involuntary exclamation of surprise and fear fell from her lips as she saw a stranger approach her.

"Ah, Miss Barnes," said Charley, as he approached and raised his hat in salutation, "I beg pardon for my intrusion; but I want to see you and your father on some very important business. Don't be alarmed Miss Barnes," he said, noticing a mild, frightened look in her eyes. "I am a friend and assure you I will do all in my power to aid you and your father."

"My father is not at home," she said, and an anxious, troubled look stole over her fair, young face. "But come in please. I was looking for father; he will be here soon."

Placing a chair for him, she went to the door and watched for her father; but he would never come again. As she watched, the sun sank slowly behind the western hills.

"Oh father!" she moaned, "why don't he come?"

"Do you know where your father went?" asked Charley.

"No," she replied, "I don't know."

"Does he often go away and leave you alone?"

"No, sir; he never did before."

"Why did he leave you alone to-day?"

"He did not intend to be gone but a few minutes; and, as I was busy with my work, I did not go with him. We are getting ready to leave here. We intend to leave to-morrow."

"If I knew where to look for him," said the detective,

"I would go and see if I could find him. Do you have any idea where he would be likely to go? Does he have any particular place where he goes in search of game?"

"Yes," she answered, "he generally goes to the 'Lick,' as he calls it."

"Perhaps that he has gone there. Tell me the way and I will go and see if I can find him," said Charley.

"I will go with you," she answered. "I am afraid to stay here alone."

"What are you afraid of?"

"I don't know," she answered, "but I am afraid that something has happened to father. He told me to-day that the Indians did not act as friendly when they came here as they used to, and he was afraid something was wrong,"

"Have you seen any Indians around here laterly?"

"Yes, there were some here yesterday."

"Ah, yes, and how many were there of them?"

"There were three."

"There were no white men with them, were there?" he asked.

"No; you are the first white man I have seen for a year. Excuse me, but I was so anxious about father that I forgot to offer you some supper. We have not much, but you are welcome; please sit up and partake of what little we have."

"Thank you, Miss Barnes; you have a plenty, I am sure. Much more and infinitely better than I am used to having. But about those Indians, Miss Barnes,—you say they have acted strange of late. Did your father know them?" ask the detective, as he seated himself at the table.

"No sir," she answered, "they were strangers."

"By ginger," he thought, "I wonder if those two devils have disguised themselves as Indians and are spying upon the old man. This is the girl that that Kingsbury and Frank have been fighting for. By thunder now, I don't wonder much at it either! I would fight for her myself. Let me see," he said aloud, you say there were three of these strangers?"

"No, father knew one of them; two were strangers."

"Two strangers," he mused, "what for looking men were they?"

"One of them was a large, heavy, rough looking man—"

"Ah!" exclaimed Charley, "and the other!"

"The other was a small, slim and rather nice looking fellow," she answered.

"You noticed him in particular, I suppose."

"Will you have another cup of coffee?" she asked, evasively.

"No, thanks—I have drinked too much already. Now, I am ready to go. You think you would know where he would be likely to go, do you?"

"Yes," she answered, as they started out together.

"By thunder!" mused Charley, as his companion led the way, "I believe that those two Indians were no other than John Barnes and Jim Kingsbury in disguise. I wonder what their game is any way? By ginger, now! is it possible that they have been watching the old man and have waylaid and, possibly, murdered him? Something is wrong, or he would have been back before now."

For half an hour, they tramped on through the dark forest, growing darker and gloomier as the shadows of night gathered around them. All nature seemed hushed in a silent and deep repose. But suddenly, out upon the still evening air, rang out clear and distinct, the report of two rifle shots, fired almost simultaneously.

Zell clutched her companion's arm and listened in breathless and eager silence. But all was still again.

"Oh, sir," cried Zell, "do you think that it was my father who fired those shots?"

"Perhaps so," said the detective, but he did not dare tell her just what he thought. "No," he thought, "he did not fire those two shots. He may have fired one of them, but not both—he couldn't have fired two shots so nearly together. Ah," he mused, "if those scoundrels have followed the old man, those shots may mean more than I would care to tell her."

By this time, they had reached the 'Lick' and had stopped and were listening in the hope of hearing some sound to guide them, when the silence was broken by the sound of voices.

—"Well, you are welcome to the girl; just manage her to suit yourself," came in the voice of John Barnes. "But I'll tell you, Jim, we have got to get out of here before the Indians find out what we have done, or they will make trouble for us. They are crazy to get possession of that diamond, and if they knew that we have got it, they would be after us."

"They won't know that we have got it, we will tell them that the old man has concealed it somewhere about the cabin. But come, let's hurry on for the Indians will be getting impatient.   They are waiting for us at the cabin by this time, and there's no telling what they may do if they find out that the old man is away."

"Now," continned Jim, "that the old man is out of the way, we will have everything all our own way.   Zell won't suspect anything, for she thinks that I am all right.   So all we have to do is to carry out our plan just as we started out.   Let the Indians attack the cabin, and carry off the girl, then we will sail in and rescue her; and then—ah, well I can persuade her.   Of course she will think that the Indians killed the old man.   It was a streak of good luck that we met him in the woods this evening, for we are rid of him and have got the diamond besides, which, if I mistake not, will be a fortune for us."

"I had no faith in that diamond story," said John; "but it is more valuable even than the stories represented it."

"Neither had I," replied Jim, "and I was willing to let the Indians have all the plunder, but we have got it, and we will keep it."

"Well," said John, "I don't know as you have any title to it; and, as you will get the girl, which was all you wanted, I think that I will lay claim to the treasure for my share of the spoils.   I am a sort of heir anyway, you know."

"Not hardly," said Jim.   "I have a much right to it as you have, and I will—"

"It makes no difference; you came here to get the girl; all plunder was to fall to me and the Indians.   I have got the stone and I will keep it!   You murdered the old man and—"

Further conversation was checked; for, as he uttered those awful words, ''You have murdered the old man,'' Zell threw up her hands and, with a low, agonized cry, fell fainting into the detective's arms.

———:o:———

CHAPTER XXI.

A NIGHT OF HORROR.

There was no time to lose, for thought or plans; for, as that agonized cry fell upon the ears of the assassins, who were scarcely fifty feet away, and who, realizing as they did from whose lips it came, dashed forward in pursuit of their victim. Well did they know that their villainous plot was known, and that nothing now remained but to capture her.

Quickly raising the girl in his arms, the detective dashed away into the forest. Darkness hid them from view, and, for a time, the sound of their pursuers guided him in his flight.

At last, from sheer exhaustion, the detective was compelled to stop. Their pursuers could still be heard, but it was plain that he had succeeded in eluding them, for the sound of footsteps passed on and soon died away in the distance.

"Ah," said Charley, kneeling down by the side of the unconscious girl, "poor child—poor little woman, we are safe for a while at least, safe till morning!" Chafing her hands and temples briskly, he soon had the satisfaction of restoring her to consciousness.

At last, she opened her eyes and looked about her in a wild and frightened manner, and moaned—

"Father! father! Oh, my God, they have murdered him!"

"Hush," said Charley, raising her to her feet, "hush, they will hear us. Cheer up; don't give up so; it may not be so bad!"

A Novel Guide.

"Oh, sir!" she moaned, "is there any hope?"

"For us there is, but I suppose your father is dead."

"Oh God!" she sobbed, "what can I do?"

"Trust to me, Miss Zell," he said, "I will protect you; as long as I have life and strength, no harm shall come to you. Come, now; can you walk!"

"Yes, I think so," she replied.

"Come then, let's get away from here. Take my arm and let me help you, Our only hope is to get away from here before morning."

For an hour, they tramped on, not knowing where they were going. The darkness had become so intense that they could no longer distinguish one another, making it almost impossible for them to pick their way through the dense forest.

Now, too, the distant rumbling of thunder told them of an approaching storm.

Dragging themselves wearily beneath the drooping branches of a spruce tree, which would shelter them from the coming storm, Charley bade his companion to lie down and rest.

"There," he said, as he wrapped his coat about her, "that will keep you warm; now go to sleep and rest if you can. You will feel better. I will watch."

For two hours, the storm raged and the girl slept. Protected from the rain by the sheltering branches overhead, and snugly and warmly wrapped in the detective's coat, the tired girl was soundly sleeping, when a vivid flash of lightning, followed by a peal of thunder which shook the mountains to their very foundations, brought the sleeping girl back from her happy dreams to the stern reality of her hard and cruel lot.

"Oh, how could I sleep," she cried, "while poor father lies dead, or dying alone in these cold, dreary woods!"

"Sh—, listen," said the detective, "I can hear something!"

Listening, they could hear the sound of footsteps; soft and low they sounded, as something cautiously approached them.

Listening, with his gun in readiness, the detective stood and watched, and waited for the intruder. Again came the sound; now, wearily approaching to within a few feet of them, then paused, as if to consider the possibilities of the situation.

"What is it?" asked Zell in low whisper, as she crouched close to Charley's side.

"It's only a bear," he said, as it's shaggy outlines became visible in the darkness. "Don't be afraid, he won't molest us, I think. He is only trying to satisfy his curiosity as to what kind of creatures we are."

Just then, a low, indistinct cry fell upon the ears of the trio. The bear seemed to be the most interested in it, for he pricked up his ears and listened intently for a repetition of the sound. It sounded a long way off; so faint, so low and indistinct, that they could not tell whether it came from human lips or from some wild animal.

The bear, after listening awhile, started off in the direction from whence the sound came. So acute of hearing, perhaps it had sounded more distinct to the bear than it had to his strange companions. At any rate, his curiosity prompted him to follow up the sound and satisfy himself as to its cause

"Come," said Charley, "as the bear started off, "let's follow after him and see what it was that made that noise. He will hunt it up." Silently, they followed after their dumb guide.

Some two hundred yards or more, they followed, when, suddenly, they came upon the bear, who, becoming dissatisfied, or from curiosity's sake, had stopped to investigate matters a little.   As they came up, he greeted them with an angry growl, as he turned and reared upon his haunches and waited as if expecting an immediate attack from the intruders.   But the detective had no desire for an encounter with Mr. Bruin.

A slight movement from the girl was greeted with an angry growl and the displaying of a set of shining ivory, while the little, black, bead-like eyes of the monster gleamed viciously upon the fair little creature whom he seemed to consider with so much fear and suspicion.

"Don't be afraid," said Charley, as the girl shrunk back from the presence of the shaggy monster, and stepped so confidently to his side.   Don't be afraid, I can kill him if I have to, but I don't want to shoot if I can help it, for the report of my gun will attract other and more dangerous enemies than he is."

Involuntarily the detective's strong right arm stole around the slender, trembling form of his little companion and drew her yielding form close to his side. Somehow, that strong, friendly embrace sent a feeling of security, a thrill of hope to the weary heart of the friendless, homeless, little orphan girl.   She felt that she could trust this great, good-natured fellow.   Instinctively, she clung to him for protection.   To this man whom, but a few hours before, she looked upon with a feeling of dread, of fear well-nigh akin to despair. As she felt the pressure of that strong, protecting arm, she raised her wild, wandering blue eyes to his and murmured—

"Oh, sir, you are so very, very kind to me and I thank you so much; but oh, I would a thousand times rather that you would let me die here in these dark, dreary forests and mountains, than for you to take me back to New York, a prisoner, to be convicted a criminal and sent to prison. Oh, that I could die here with my father and forever bury with us that miserable crime—a crime that has haunted me day and night ever since the fatal work was done! Oh, I know, my heart tells me you are a detective and have hunted me down to drag me back to be punished for my crime! Yes, I am guilty, I forged the checks! Oh, I have dreamed of this—dreamed that I was dragged away from my father by the hand of strangers. But, alas! I have no right to ask for mercy; I am guilty; take me and do with me as you will—I am your prisoner!"

"No, no; don't talk so, my little friend. You are not my prisoner. I have not come here to arrest you. Trust me, little woman, for I am your friend; and so long as God gives me life and strength, I will honor and protect yon, so have no fear of me. You are just as safe with me as you would be with your own father, perhaps safer, for I am better able to protect you against your enemies here than he was. I know the story of that forgery, and I know whose hand it was that did the deed. It was not your fault, you but obeyed the request of your father in doing the work; you are not responsible for your act."

"Oh, sir!" murmured the girl in the gratefulness of her heart, "you are so kind, so generous; perhaps too much so, for others may not see and understand my guilt as you do. But, to whom am I indebted for all this generous kindness, and the hope that it brings to my aching heart?"

"Charley Shipton is my name. I am a detective, and I am off on a summer's vacation, but I came here to find you and your father. But, I surpose, your father is dead; you are but a girl, and I am free to act as I please; so you may depend upon it. I will do nothing that will cause you to regret my coming."

"Oh, thank you, sir! exclaimed Zell, thankfully.

"Hark, did you hear anything?" asked Charley.

"No, but see, the bear acts as if he heard something."

"Here it is again!"

"Oh sir," cried Zell, "do you think that it might be my father?"

"I don't know," he replied, but he dared not tell her what he thought; for it was in that vicinity that those two shots were fired which had attracted their attention in the evening. Knowing, as he did, after hearing the conversation of the two assassins, that they had met and shot the girl's father, he believed that that cry he had heard and which had attracted the bear's attention, was her father's.

Shot down and left to die, he had, in his agony, uttered the cry which they had heard. Believing this, and kuowing the natural instinct of the bear would lead him to the object, whatever it might be, Charley had followed, in the hope of finding the murdered man.

Again, the bear, who had remained so long inactive, as if studying and trying to satisfy his curiosity as to the nature of his visitors, began to show signs of uneasiness, by pointing his nose in the direction from which the sound had come, and sniffing like a hungry dog that scents food.

Just then, out upon the still morning air came a low moan, followed by the one word—''Zell.''

With a glad cry, Zell darted forward, heedless of the great, shaggy beast, who stood almost in her path and nearly running against the bear in her eager haste.

''Father, father!'' she called, as she ran swiftly in the direction from whence the sound had come.

Walking cautiously around the bear, Charley soon came upon a scene that would have softened a harder heart than his.

Down upon the cold, wet ground, with her dying father's head pillowed upon her throbbing bosom, sat Zell, crying and sobbing piteously.

With bowed and bared head the detective stood and watched the sad scene of a dying father who, with a feeble, faltering voice, was praying God to protect his child whom he, so soon, would be compelled to leave to the mercy of a stranger, away in the far off forests of Montana.

Fainter and fainter grew the feeble, faltering accents. But rallying a little, he turned his wistful gaze upon the detective.

"Let me examine your wound first," said Charley, kneeling by his side.

"It's no use, said the dying man, as the detective, with skillful fingers, bandaged the wound in his side.

"I'm going fast, and oh, so soon must I leave my darling child with you! Tell me, oh tell me that you will take her—that you will protect her from the villain who is seeking her ruin; who would drag her down to a life of shame and wretchedness. Tell me that you will love her, that you will honor her as a sister! Tell me; it is the prayer of a dying father! May God help you, my children!"

"The white-haired head of the dying father drooped lower and lower upon the throbbing bosom, the sad eyes closed, and, in a moment, like a child in a mother's arms, he rested in peace.

"Zell," said Charley, gently removing the father's head from her bosom and laying him down, "your father is dead. Zell," he continued, "the prayer of your dying father shall be answered, so far as I am able. And here, over his dead body and before God, do I vow to avenge his death, to love and protect his child, God help me!"

With blanched cheek, white and compressed lips, Zell arose and stretching out her hand, so small, white and all stained with the life-blood of her father—the blood, which she so vainly tried to stop by pressing her hand upon his wounded side—to the detective, and, over her dead father, she said—

"Oh sir! you are so kind, so generous—God grant that I may prove worthy of so noble a friend! Take me, poor, wretched girl that I am, and I will love and obey you as your own child!"

Thus standing—hands clasped in hands, over the dead body of her father—as they uttered these words, they heard the sound of approaching footsteps, followed by a shout of triumph from the two assassins, who, followed by the six Indians, whom they had hired to aid them in their fiendish work, appeared upon the scene.

————:O:————

CAPTIVITY.

CHAPTER XXII.

In a moment the detective was overpowered, and with hands bound behind him, he was led away by the Indians, followed by Kingsbury, leading his captive, Zell.

For two days, they tramped through the forests and mountains and, at last, arrived at the Indian village, where the half-breed and his savage companions lived. It was a village of some fifty or more inhabitants. Miserable, degraded creatures, who lived by making thieving depredations npon the white settlers of the surrounding country. A fit place for the committing of a dark and shameless crime.

The detective was dragged through the miserable village, followed by a crowd of dirty urchins and amid the shouts and jeers of hideous squaws, who had been told that the prisoner was a detective and had come to arrest the young men for stealing horses.

Grand were the preparations and high the drunken carnival of that evening; for, on the morrow, at sunrise, the captive detective was to be burned at the stake. Kingsbury and Barnes had declared that it would not be safe for them to keep him any longer and urged the execution.

Everything was ready, and the detective, bound hand and foot, was left tied to a tree for the night.

As he stood thus, musing upon his almost hopeless condition and upon the awful fate that awaited the helpless girl, the rustle of a light footstep sounded close and a low, sweet voice whispered in his ear—

(139)

"Ah, the pale face dog shall die, and he ought! My people wronged him not; he had no business to come here!"

"Oh!" exclaimed Charley, as he beheld the graceful form of a young Indian maiden, who looked upon him as an enemy who deserved his fate. "And pray, m pretty little maid, who are you?"

"The fawn," she replied.

"Have you seen the white girl?" asked Charley anxiously.

"The White Lily? no I have not. I will go and see her. They said that you killed her father and were carrying her away to be your slave. Oh, what a wicked man!"

"But they lied to you, little Fawn; I never did it! They have lied to your people! Go and ask the white girl, she will tell you."

"Ah, I will go to her," and in a moment she was gone.

As Zell was brought to the village, she was taken to a hut and placed in care of an old squaw, who was told to guard her closely and allow no one to see her.

Here, guarded by the old hag, she was left till after the council which was held to try the prisoner. After the council had found the prisoner guilty and had condemned him to be burned at sunrise on the following morning, Kingsbury went to the hut. Entering, he approached the horrified girl and said—

"Zell, there's no use of tears, of prayers, or anything of the kind. This night, you shall be my wife. The wedding ceremony, according to the custom of this village, has already been performed. Nothing is left, but

for me to claim my bride, and I swear by the God whom
you believe and trust in, that, unless you consent and
yield yourself to me this night, your friend shall die at
sunrise in the morning. I have offered you all that
anyone can offer: I have offered you wealth, position,
love, in fact everything that heart could wish, but you
have spurned me. Now, you are in my power, and this
night you shall be my bride. As for myself, there's
nothing to be said; your own conscience is not clear;
for a word from me would send you to prison for at
least twenty years or more. Ah, you may well turn
pale and tremble at the thought! Choose then, shall
your friend go free? will you consent to be my wife and
let your friend live, or will you refuse and thus condemn
your friend to die? Choose! for in an hour I will return
and claim my bride."

A few minutes after he had left the hut, the Fawn
entered, and going up to the weeping girl, she said in
her soft, sweet voice—

"Ah, the White Lily is sad!"

"Yes," said Zell; and in a few minutes she had told
the Fawn the story of her captivity.

"The treacherous dog!" cried the Fawn; and her
black eyes blazed with indignation. "He has lied to
my people! The White Lilies friend shall not die!" And
in a moment more, the Fawn had glided as swiftly and
silently away, as she had entered.

· It was midnight, dark and gloomy, and the detective
was lying awake and thinking. He thought of his friends
and wondered, if they would ever know of the sad ending of his summer's vacation. He thought of the poor
girl, whom he had sworn to love and protect, and his

heart bled for her; for he knew, all but too well, the sad fate, a thousand times worse than his own, that awaited her.

Oh, my God," he moaned, "must I remain here and allow that fiendish devil to accomplish his hellish desire! Oh God, I can't—I won't allow—"

"Sh—" came in a low whisper close to his ear, and a knife flashed before his eyes and, in a moment, he was free.

"Ah," whispered that same soft, sweet voice, "the pale-face is not the dog I believed him," said the Fawn. "I saw the White Lily and she told me. Go now," she said; "the White Lily is in trouble." And in a moment she was gone.

Listening to the retreating footsteps of the Fawn, the detective's quick ear caught the sound of another footstep. Were the movements of the Fawn discovered? Listening, Charley soon saw that the midnight prowler was going in the direction of the hut where Zell was confined. Following silently, Charley saw the dark form pause for a moment before the door of the hut to assure himself that all was well, then the dark form entered.

"Ah," muttered the detective, "thank God, I am not too late!"

And crawling swiftly to the door, he heard the pleading voice of Zell. She was pleading for his life.

"To save his life, oh God!" she wailed, "I will be your wife."

"Good!" cried the villain, in a tone of triumph, as

he advanced toward the horrified girl with outstretched arms. "My bride, my—"

The sentence was never finished, for at that instant, the door was burst open and the detective, with a bound like an enraged lion, sprang upon the cowering villain and dealt him a blow with his iron fist, that felled him bruised and bleeding to the ground.

Quick as lightning, Charley seized the fainting girl in his arms and turned toward the door.

"Halt!" commanded John Barnes, barring the way. The command was followed by the ominous click of his revolvers, while behind him was seen the hideous, painted faces of a score of Indians. "Halt! Move a hand, and you are a dead man!"

———:o:———

CHAPTER XX III.

Hardly had the words escaped his lips. when the detective sprang upon him, dealing him a blow that laid him stunned and bleeding at his feet. Seizing the revolvers, the detective discharged them into the faces of the Indians, he rushed out of the hut and was gone before they had sufficiently recovered to intercept his flight.

"Stop him, stop him!" yelled Jim Kingsbury, staggering to his feet, but it was too late.

"By thunder!" muttered Charley, "as he dashed away into the woods, "I think that that dose will satisfy him for a day or two, at least. By jinks, now, he won't feel like bothering the girl again for a while."

A little later the Fawn entered the hut, an approaching Zell, said—

"Ah, the White Lily's friend has avenged her insult. The Fawn will stay with her to-night, and she will be safe. The pale-face dare not come here while Fawn is here."

For two days Zell had not even seen Kingsbury, a thing for which she could not be grateful enough.

"No," laughed the Fawn, "he is not in a very presentable condition at present. He will not bother you again, for some time at least."

"Do they know where my friend is?" asked Zell of her new friend, as they lay down together upon their hard bed for the night.

"Oh yes, they know, they don't have to hunt to find

(144)

THE FLIGHT.

him. He is only a little way off, so, if you were to cry
for help, he would hear you. I saw him yesterday, and
again to-day; but I am afraid of him, and I dare not go
near him. Ah, but he is a noble brave, though he is a
white man, and so strong. No two, nor three of the
strongest warriors dare fight him. He will come for you
by and by, for he loves the White Lily. Ah, your
cheeks blush crimson—you love him! Tell me, White
Lily, do the pale-faces love as we do?"

"I don't know," murmured Zell. And for a long time
she lay thinking of her friend. But, at last, tired nature
closed her eyes in sleep.

How long she had slept, she knew not, when she was
awakened suddenly; for something had touched her face.
She tried to call to her sleepiug friend, but a heavy hand
was quickly placed over her mouth and a voice whispered in her ear—

"Zell, it is Charley—come let's go."

Silently, and without a murmur, she arose and followed him. Out into the darkness, out into the night,
they crept. They had passed the outskirts of the village
and had almost reached the forest, whose dark, gloomy
shadows would have shielded them from view and enabled them to make good their escape, when, unfortunately for them, the Indian maden awoke and missed her
companion. Fearing that something had happened to
the girl, the Fawn rushed out and aroused the people.
In an instant the Indians and the two white men were
in pursuit. They saw the fugitives, as they hurried
away toward the forest, and gave chase. In a few
minutes the Indians overtook them and, after a short

but desperate struggle, overpowered the dauntless detective and brought them back to the village.

The next morning a council was held and, after a long and stormy debate, in which money and whiskey were used to persuade the Indians and to influence them to decide against the captive, again the detective was condemned to be burned at the stake at an early hour the following morning.

It was a day of rejoicing, and late into the night the wild orgies lasted.

All preparations for the execution had been made. The stake set, the fagots heaped about it and the detective, bound hand and foot, dragged forth and placed upon the pile. To make him doubly secure, he was bound to the stake with an extra rope and a guard placed over him.

Till after midnight the night was made hideous by the drunken revelries of these human fiends, when, becoming tired and stupid from dancing and drinking, the crowd gradually dwindled away, till only the guard, placed to watch the prisoner, remained.

An hour passed, when the guard, who had been pacing back and forth before the captive, becoming tired, and feeling, no doubt, that there was no possibility of the prisoner escaping, had sat down a few paces away, to rest.

Five, ten minutes passed, and still the guard sat quietly.

A light rustling in the bushes close by attracted the detective's attention. Listening intently, he heard a light, stealthy footstep approaching, but whether of friend or foe, he could not tell, as the moon had gone down, leaving all shrouded in impenetrable darkness.

On came the creeping sound.

Bound hand and foot and totally unable to move, he lay and listened to the stealthy approach with a feeling of horror.

Unable to defend himself, he would fall an easy victim to the enemy, if such he be.

"But then," he mused, "why should I fear? Why should a few short hours' lease of life seem so precious to one condemned to die? But how selfish! Thinking only of myself, when poor, little Zell will suffer a thousand times worse than I. How gladly would she exchange her fate for mine!"

Nearer and nearer came that creeping sound; till, at last, it paused directly at his side. There was a fumbling among the fagots; a scratching sound, as if some one was lighting a match.

"Great heavens," thought the horrified captive, "can it be possible that Kingsbury, anxious to be rid of me, has come and is applying the match with his own hand, so as to make sure of his victim?"

Oh the horror of that moment! Already, in his horrified imagination, the detective could hear the crackling flames. For the first time in his varied career, the detective gave up in despair. All hope had fled.

"Oh my God!" he moaned aloud, "that I could live long enough to make one more attempt to save poor, little Zell!"

"Charley," came in a whisper soft and low, so close to his cheek, that her warm breath fanned his hot cheek, "Charley, it is I—Zell."

"Oh, thank God?" he murmured.

With eager, trembling hand, she loosened the rope that bound his hands, and then he was soon free.

With an inexpressible feeling of joy he arose to his feet, and clasping the brave, little woman in his strong arms, he pressed her to his heart and whispered—

"Zell—my brave little girl!"

"Charley!" she murmured.

"Come," whispered Charley; and he led her away— away into the darkness, beyond the village and into the dark, gloomy woods.

On, on, they hurried. Two hours had passed and then, just as the sun rose above the hill-tops—the hour of his execution — the sound of men in pursuit was heard.

"Oh Charley," cried Zell in despair, "leave me and save yourself; you can't help me! You are unarmed and they will kill you this time. Leave me, Charley, leave—"

"Never!" cried Charley. "I will never leave you! By heaven," he hissed, "you are mine and the devils of hell can't take you away from me! Oh that I had my gun! Come. come," he urged; "can't you go any further, Zell?"

"I am afraid, not," she panted. "Oh Charley, leave me and save yourself; please do! for you can do me no good by staying with me. Make your escape, you can get away; then, perhaps, you may be able to save me—"

"Never!" he cried. "I can't do it—I won't do it, by heaven I won't! Jim Kingsbury shall not have you again—"

"O look! look!" cried Zell. "There they are. Quick, Charley, leave—"

With a wild yell of defiance, Charley caught the slight, girlish form up in his arms and bounded away through the woods, while the Indians, urged on by Kingsbury and Barnes, started in pursuit.

The fugitives had crossed a little brook and were running along the base of a high bluff, when Kingsbury and a half dozen Indians appeared directly in their path.

"Now," cried the detective, placing his burden upon her feet, "we are in for it!"

Before them, to the right of them and behind them, came the yelling savages. In front of them came Jim Kingsbury; running up to within fifty yards, he stopped, raised his rifle and took deliberate aim at the broad breast of the detective.

His finger was already pressing the trigger, when Zell, with a cry of terror, sprang between them, shielding him with her own body.

Thwarted in his attempt to shoot the detective, Kingsbury uttered a horrible oath, and again sprang forward.

"Let us try once more, Zell," cried Charley, seizing her hand and dragging her mercilessly through a clump of bushes toward the bluff.

————:o:————

CHAPTER XXIV.

LOST IN THE CAVERN.

With torn clothes, bruised and bleeding flesh, they forced their way through the thicket and stood at the foot of the bluff. It was a last desperate effort to escape.

Directly before them, in the face of the cliff, was a dark hole which appeared to be an entrance to a cave. Without considering whether it offered them hope of escape or whether it was luring them into a trap, the detective raised the girl in his strong arms and darted forward and entered the cave, just as their pursuers burst through the thicket in pursuit.

Down into the depths of the dark and unknown cavern he hurried, bearing his precious burden, knowing nothing and caring but little where he was going, so he escaped his pursuers. Could he have known the suffering that awaited them there, he might have paused before going far; but he did not know—he could not see—he only knew that he must escape, and here was his only hope.

Behind them they could hear their pursuers, before them all was darkness and uncertainty; but on, still on, they hurried, till at last, exhausted, he was compelled to stop.

All was still and so dark that they could not see one another. Their pursuers had either given up the chase or had lost them in the darkness.

"Zell," whispered Charley, as he removed his coat and wrapped it about her shoulders, "lie down and try to rest. I will watch."

FORCING THE WAY THROUGH THE THICKET.

Weary and worn by her long flight and sleepless nights, the poor girl was soon asleep.

For an hour or more the detective watched; but hearing no sigh of their pursuers, he concluded, that they had given up the pursuit and were, probably, awaiting the return of the fugitives at the mouth of the cave.

"Well," he muttered, "you can well afford to wait, for we will have to return before long.

"Poor girl!" he said, as he sat down and, raising her head from the damp, cold rocks, rested it upon his lap, "that is a hard bed. There," he mused, "that is better." And he gently smoothed back the damp curls from her brow.

For hours he sat thus, thinking of the events of the past few days; so strange, it almost seemed a dream, a romance, such as he had read of in novels. Yet, stranger than fiction were the trying events of the past few days. Thus he sat, thinking for how long, he knew not, for his thoughts gave way to dreams.

He was dreaming of home and friends, when he was aroused from his slumbers by a gentle shake, and a low voice whispered—

"Charley, I can hear something; wake up, it is coming this way!"

In an instant he was awake and listening, but all was still again. Whatever it was that the girl had heard, had either gone back or passed on without molesting them.

"I wonder how long we have been here, Zell?" asked Charley. "It was about sunrise, when we came in— about five o'clock, I think."

"I have got my watch," replied Zell, "so if you have got a match, we can soon tell."

Matches are indispensible to one upon a summer's vacation to the mountains, camping out, and fishing, and hunting, and producing one, he lighted and held it to the face of the little watch. It was just ten minutes past six.

"We have been here a little over an hour," said Zell.

"An hour!" exclaimed Charley, "thirteen of them, Zell; by ginger!"

"Impossible, Charley!" she exclaimed, "I don't believe that we have been here so long. But what shall we do? I am rested now, and so thirsty! Can't we find some water?"

"I don't know," he answered, "we will try. Let's go and perhaps we will be fortunate enough to find some before long."

And so they set out, but to where or what, they knew not.

On, on, in the darkness, they picked their way. Hour after hour passed, till the night had chased away the day, and, again the day had dispelled the night; but it was all darkness to them. Their suffering had become almost intolerable. Dragging themselves wearily along, they strove, but it seemed to them in vain, to escape their gloomy prison. At last, completely overcome by fatigue, they were compelled to stop.

"Zell," said Charley, "we are lost; we will gain nothing by wandering aimlessly about; sit down and rest, if you can."

And again wrapping his coat about her, he sat down and resting her head upon his lap, he sat for hours by the sleeping girl, vainly striving to devise some plan of escape. Vain indeed were his plans; for, what could he do, what could he hope? Evidently something must be done before long, or they must certainly perish from hunger and thirst.

"Zell," said Charley, as he could endure her pitiful moaning no longer, "wake up!" And he shook her gently. But a low moan was her only answer.

"Oh God!" he moaned, as he raised the limp and almost lifeless form in his arms, "she is dying!" Staggering on in the darkness, he resolved to make one more desperate effort to escape. Oh the horror of that hour of gloom! But at last, exhausted, he stopped, and laying his burden down, he knelt beside her.

"Charley," she murmured, "I had such a sweet dream—I dreamt that I was with father and he took me in his arms and carried me home to mother. Oh, we were so happy, and the good things we had to eat; and oh! the cool, sweet water I drank. But, oh Charley! it was all a dream; and I am so thirsty, so—so hungry!"

"Sh—, listen," interrupted Charley, "I can hear something; it is coming this way!"

Listening they could hear the stealthy approach of some animal.

"What is it? What does he intend to do?" were questions which crowded through the minds of the fugitives, as they listened to that slow, stealthy approach. Nearer and nearer he came, creeping slowly, cautiously toward them.

"Oh, that I had a gun or something to defend ourselves with!" exclaimed the detective. "Feeble as such
a defense must necessarily be, it would be far better
than to remain, like two terror-stricken children, unable
to resist."

"Light a match, Charley," whispered Zell. "Haven't
you got some paper, or something that will burn? Wild
animals are afraid of fire."

"Ah, my note-book!" exclaimed the detective. "But
it is precious, I hate to lose it; but life is more precious."

And in a moment the precious note-book was ignited.
At the first flash of the flames of the burning memo-
randum which dispelled the darkness around them, was
revealed to their horrified gaze a sight, which, though
they might live a hundred years, they could never
forget.

Before them, and not ten feet away, with lowered
head and crouching form, stood a huge, vicious looking
beast. Crouching, ready for the fatal spring, his wicked
green eyes glaring vindictively upon them, he stood for
one awful moment.

————:o:————

HONOR AMONG THIEVES.

CHAPTER XXV.

TRAPPED.

,,After them!" yelled Kingsbury, as the detective, with Zell in his arms, disappeared within the cave. And dashing forward, he discharged his gun at the fugitives.

"Trapped, by George!" shouted John Barnes. "Trapped, like a rat in a hole! By thunder, we'll have them now!"

An hour later, when they returned from their fruitless search, they were not so confident that their game was trapped.

"No use of following them in there," said Kingsbury; "we will just wait here till they come back. We'll starve them out. They can't stand it very long without anything to eat."

"Do you know this place, Frenchy, asked John of the half-breed.

"No," he replied, "I never was here before."

"Is there any other place where they can get out of here?" asked Jim of one of the Indians.

"No," he replied, "no get out any place else; have to come back here soon. Heap big cave. May be they get lost and no find the way back here. Ugh!" he said, with a shrug of the shoulder, "heap bad place; mountain lions live in there—ugh!"

"I am not so sure of this thing, Jim," said John, after waiting for two days; "but I don't know as it matters much, so we get rid of that devil of a detective, whether he comes back or not. Just so he can't get out any other way, we will be all right, so let them starve to death in there if they want to."

(155)

"But that won't answer my purpose," said Jim. "We must search for them."

"We no wait much longer," declared the chief of the Indians; "we go to find 'Great Medicine-stone'. Old man hid him in cabin, we find him."

"No," said Jim, "the girl knows where it is hid. We must catch her or we can't find it."

"Whag!" grunted the Indian disdainfully, "we catch him once, and she no tell!"

"Let them go," said John Barnes, "we don't need them. One of us can watch here while the other one goes in and searches for them. You go in and search for them and I will stay here and watch, so they can't escape," said John, and there was a cunning, treacherous look in his evil eyes.

"No," said Jim, not daring to trust his partner in crime. "No, you go first and let me stay; or give me the diamond and let me go first—just as you please." Two scheming, treacherous villains, neither dared to trust the other with the valuable treasure which they had stolen.

"I will go first," growled John. And there was an ugly gleam in his sinister eyes as he prepared to go. "Curse you, Jim Kingsbury," he muttered, "my time will come next." Armed with torch and his pockets full of leaves to mark the trail, so he would not get lost in the cave and to avoid searching the same ground over twice, he entered the cavern to search for the lost fugitives, bearing the precious stone with him.

"Trust him!" muttered Jim, as John disappeared down into the dark and unknown depths of the cavern. "Trust him, not I!"

After a long and fruitless search, John returned from the cave and reported, that he had traced them for miles down into the very heart of the mountain, and then had lost all trace of them. So, then, he took his turn at the watch, while Jim went in to search, taking the diamond with him, as John had done.

"Curse you!" hissed John Barnes, as Kingsbury disappeared in the cave. "By thunder! you shall never leave that cave alive! You would not hesitate to take my life for that gem, nor will I hesitate to take yours. I have murdered one man for it now; another won't make but a little difference."

And uttering these horrible words, he secreted himself in the dark passage and, revolver in hand, ready for instant use, he awaited the return of Kingsbury.

"Yes, yes," he muttered, "I will kill him, and then the stone will be all my own. The Indians know nothing of our having it, and will suspect nothing. I will tell them that it was a mistake—that I thought he was the detective."

But he was destined to be disappointed in his murderous plan. For fifteen hours he waited and watched, but Jim did not come.

"What does it mean?" muttered Barnes. "Curse him, I say! Is it possible that he has discovered some other way to get out of the cave? No, no; that is impossible," he thought, "but perhaps something has happened to him."

Calling to the Indians, who were camped close by, he questioned them closely in regard to the cave and whether there was any other cave in the vicinity and was horrified on learning that there was another cave close by; though the Indians declared that it was not connected with the one he was watching.

"How in thunder do you know?" yelled Barnes, fairly livid with rage and fear. "Curse you, you stupid idiots, show me the place, quick! O curse you, Jim Kingsbury! If you have escaped from the cave and have run away, I will follow you to the ends of the earth and kill you!"

In a few minutes they reached the other cave; and, after a careful examination, he was satisfied that no one had gone out or in there. The entrance was small and the ground sandy, so, that if any one had passed that way, their footprints would have been easily seen.

"Well, it's all right," he muttered, "but it might have been otherwise. No, nothing has been here except some animal."

"Ugh!" grunted the Indian, "heap big mountain lion." And he pointed to the tracks in the sand.

————:o:————

THE MOUNTAIN LION.

CHAPTER XXVI.

SAVED.

As it will be remembered, we left Charley and Zell confronting the huge brute—a mountain lion, and one of the largest of his kind—waiting for him to spring upon them. Retreat was impossible, resistance was equally hopeless. In a moment such an unequal contest must terminate fatally to the heroic detective; for, so weak and feeble from starvation and thirst, he could make but a feeble resistance against the powerful teeth and claws of the vicious brute.

In a moment, and it seemed to them, just at the instant when the great beast was about to spring upon them, an unlooked for incident, or providence, as the case may be, entirely changed the aspect of affairs. For at that moment the leaves of the burning note-book, which formed their impromptu torch and which, in a moment more, would be consumed, again leaving our friends in darkness, suddenly parted, causing the flames to flare up brightly for a few moments. The huge brute, as if seized with some sudden fear, dropped his head and tail and with a sullen, surly look in his eyes, turned and slunk slowly and sulkily away.

"Come Zell," whispered Charley, "let's follow him; perhaps he will, like the bear, lead us to something."

"Oh, if he would guide us out of here," murmured Zell. "Who can tell, perhaps God has sent him to lead us back to the world again, to life, to liberty!"

"And, perhaps to death, or worse, to captivity," said Charley; "but come!"

And he half carried, half dragged, the almost helpless

(159)

girl, as he followed the retreating footsteps of the animal. Guided by the sound of his heavy feet upon the pebbly floor of the cave, he had no difficulty in following for a considerable distance. The great brute did not seem to quite like the turn affairs had taken, but still he ambled on.

It was a desperate act on the part of the detective, but is was also a desperate case which prompted it; and, it is said, that desperate cases demand desperate remedies—so in this. It was their only hope. Like a drowning man grasping at a straw, they seized in their despair, hoping and praying for the better.

For several minutes they followed him, when, tiring of their company, or becoming alarmed at their persistance, he bounded away and left them.

But his guidance had proved their salvation; for, after following on in the direction which he had taken, for some time, they came to a little stream of cool, sparkling water, which trickled down from among the rocks and crossed their path.

"Oh, how sweet!" murmured Zell, as her parched lips kissed the cool, life-giving water.

"Hello, by ginger!" exclaimed the detective, as he stumbled and fell over some object lying upon the ground. "By jinks, Zell," he said excitedly, after feeling of the object, "it's some animal; a deer, by ginger, that that lion has brought and has been eating.

Lighting a match, he found, it was as he suspected, the half eaten remains of a large buck, still warm.

"Oh, but this is fortunate!" exclaimed Charley. "Here, Zell," he said, as he stripped the tender, juicy flesh from the body; "eat it; it is good."

She needed no second invitation, and it was not long till they had eaten all that they dared at that time. Once their terrible thirst and hunger satisfied, they lay down and were soon asleep.

Charley had been thinking of his little companion, of her hardships and sufferings, and of the strange chance which had brought them together; of the many queer haps and mishaps of his summer's vacation and wondering, how it would all end, when sleep stole over him and led him away into the land of dreams.

He dreamed of a little home somewhere, and he saw the sweet, beautiful face of his little companion there, surrounded by a troop of bright-eyed children, who ran to meet him with glad, joyful greetings of love and kisses.

"Oh, what a happy dream! But alas! so soon to end —or at least for the present—for, as he stretched out his arms, in his dream, to clasp his smiling, happy wife to his heart, a low, sweet voice whispered in accents of joy and surprise—

"Oh Charley, look, look! The sun is shining! Oh, thank God, we are saved, we are saved!"

"Springing to his feet, Charley saw the bright sun shining through a small opening in the wall of their prison. But that was not all he saw; for almost at the same instant he saw something else, not quite so well calculated to inspire him with hope. It was the form of a man, and in his outstretched hand was a revolver, pointing directly at the detective's breast.

Quick as lightning the detective sprang aside. Almost simultaneously with his movement, came a blinding flash and a deafening report, and a pistol ball grazed the detective's cheek and flattened itself upon the opposite wall.

Before the smoke had passed away sufficiently for the assassin to see the effect of his shot, the detective was upon him. Then followed a struggle, fierce and awful to the poor girl who, praying for her friend, was kneeling close by.

Weak from his long fasting and exhausted by the severe strain upon his nerves that he had endured, he was at last overcome and borne to the ground.

With his knees upon the detective's chest, Kingsbury, who, searching in the cave, had come upon their trail and followed them up, coming upon them just at the moment when Charley saw him, grasped his hunting knife, raised it aloof and, with a low, triumphant oath, he hissed—

"Curse you, you detective dog! Curse you, I say; and die like a—"   .

A blinding flash, almost in his face, followed by the sharp report of a pistol, cut his sentence short, while the knife dropped from his fingers and his arm, broken near the wrist, dropped by his side. With a terrible oath he sprang to his feet and attempted to escape; but in an instant the detective was upon him and delt him a blow which sent him reeling against the wall where he sunk in a heap upon the ground.

"Curse you, Jim Kingsbury," cried Charley, taking the smoking revolver from Zell's hand, "you have just one minute to live! say your prayers."

And he pressed the cold muzzle of the pistol against the temple of the shivering, cringing wretch.   .

"Oh Charley," cried Zell, "please don't shoot him! Oh, I can't bear to see you kill him!" pleaded the tender-hearted girl.

"Just as you say, Zell," said Charley, placing the pistol in his pocket.

"Thank you, Charley," she said, with a grateful look from her dark, blue eyes.

"Come," he said, drawing her arm through his and leading her out into the bright, warm sunshine. The warm, balmy air gave them new life, new hope, as they fled away into the forest.

————:o:————

CHAPTER XXVII.

MEANTIME.

After satisfying himself that no one had gone out of the cave, Barnes went back to his old post and watched impatiently for another hour.

"Curse the luck anyway," he muttered; "why don't that infernal rascal come back? What in — can be keeping him so long ?

"Here, Frenchy! Go down into the cave and see if you can find him; and two of you fellows go and watch the other cave. Ah, what was that?" he asked. "It sounded like a pistol shot! Are there any of the Indians out hunting?"

"Yes," replied Strong Bear, a young chief, some are out hunting."

"Well, go and set some one to watch at the other cave. Now Frenchy, if you are ready," said Barnes, "go in and see if you can find Jim. Take the first passage to the right, that was the one that Jim was to take."

"All right," said the half-breed and disappeared within the cave. Hardly was he out of sight, when Barnes, hearing the report of another pistol shot, called—

"Ho! there's that shooting again. Here Frenchy, ho!" he shouted down into the cave, "come back here!"

In a moment or two the half-breed appeared at the mouth of the cave.

"What is it? he enquired; "what you want now?"

"Go down to the camp and stop those crazy fools

THE INFURIATED VILLAINS·

from shooting any more. What in thunder do they mean anyway?" he fumed.

In a few minutes Frenchy returned in haste, exclaiming excitedly—

"Nobody shoot down there; they think 'twas me!"

"Thunder and blitzen!" yelled Barnes excitedly. "What does it mean? Has Mr. Strong Bear gone over to the other cave?" he asked.

"No, he just go," replied Frenchy.

"Just go! thunder—," and he ripped out a string of oaths, blue and singeing, "what does the lazy hound mean? Curse him, I say; I'll— but here he comes.

"Ho there, speak! what's up?" cried the infuriated Barnes, as the Indian came running up.

"Squaw-girl and brave gone!" cried the Indian. "White brother Jim shoot in him arm; heap bad hurt, come!" he said, and darted swiftly back toward the cave.

Raging and cursing in his fury, Barnes followed the Indian back to the cave.

There, upon the floor of the cavern, groaning and cursing in his fury and pain, lay Kingsbury, where he had fallen. One bone of his forearm was broken and the pain was so intense as to nearly drive him frantic.

"What in thunder does this mean?" fairly howled the exasperated Barnes, as he entered the cave and advanced to where Kingsbury was laying.

"Mean!" hissed the villain, livid with pain and rage. "Mean! By the eternal, man, what can it mean! It means that I am used up and they have escaped. After

them, after them, quick!" he shouted, "they are not far
yet! Oh, dast the blundering luck!"

"But the diamond," said Barnes, "where is the stone?
Is it safe?"

"Yes," replied Kingsbury, feeling for the stone; I—
I—" he stammered, feeling in first one pocket and then
another without finding it.

"Speak," cried Barnes, "curse you, Jim Kingsbury,
curse you, I say; have you lost that stone? Don't you
try to steal it, or, by the eternal, I will kill you in a
minute! Oh what a fool I was to trust it to you!"

"I must have dropped it in the fight," said Kingsbury;
"I had it just a few minutes before. Look about the
cave and see if you can't find it. I know that the detective could not have got it."

But search as they would, the precious treasure, that
had been baptized in the life-blood of many human
beings, was not to be found.

"I must have dropped it somewhere about here, for I
had it when I came up to that entrance there. It is
somewhere between here and there," declared Kingsbury.

"Oh, they have got it fast enough," cried Barnes.
"If you dropped it, that girl must have seen it and
picked it up before she left the cave. Curse the luck,
anyway!" he groaned, as he turned from the cave and
followed the trail of the fugitives.

Making his way along as fast as he could, aided by the
Indians, after he had had his wounded arm attended to,
Kingsbury followed upon the trail and soon overtook
those who had gone on before. The trail was dim and

in some places could not be found at all, making it very slow work to follow the fugitives. But the eagle-eyed savages, like a pack of hounds, followed on. All day they followed, slowly but surely gaining upon the fugitives.

At evening they stopped to rest and to eat their scanty supper. Here Kingsbury had his wounded arm attended to again. Though it pained him considerably, he managed to bear up under it; and by the aid of a little stimulant, and the help of a couple of the Indians, to keep up with the rest.

"Confound it!" mused Barnes, "I don't know whether to believe him or not about that fight and losing the stone! If that detective done him up as he says he did, why the devil didn't he finish him while he was at it? But I will see—I will watch him. If he has lied about it, he has hid the stone and I will have to watch him to find it. Hang the luck, I ought to have kept it when I had it! What's the use of fooling with that girl? I won't do it anymore; if Jim wants her, he can get her; I won't help him. Oh, if I had only done as I ought, I might have been away from here and had the stone too. Curse it! that's what one gets for being ticklish about principle. I will take no such chances again, blame me if I do! Ah, here comes Jim now. Well," he inquired, as Jim came up to where he was sitting, "how do you feel by this time?"

"I feel as though I would like to get a shot at that fool detective!" replied Jim angrily. "Nothing would suit me better just now."

"How did it happen that he shot you, anyhow?" demanded Barnes, who was determined to have an explanation of the matter, for he did not believe the story. "You say that you had him down and was about to knife him. I'll tell you what's the matter, Jim, I believe it's a little mixed about that shooting story anyway, blame me, if I don't now!"

"I wish to heaven it had been you instead of me, then perhaps you would know all you want to about it!" cried Jim in a rage.

"Yes, I would, no doubt, know all about where that diamond is. I don't believe that you lost it at all! But I want to tell you, Jim Kingsbury, you don't want to try any of your tricks on this child. I know that the detective did not shoot you. He would never have gone off and left you while there was a spark of life in your body. I can't understand, how you could lose that diamond!"

"Neither can I; but it is very evident, to me at least, that I did lose it. As for the shooting, it is sufficient for me to know that I was shot. I dropped my pistol and, either the detective or the girl, picked it up and shot me. I couldn't tell which one did it. But I know that the girl persuaded him not to blow my brains out, for he meant to do it."

"She was a blamed fool! I say that much for her. Probably she picked up the 'stone' too."

"Ah, here comes the scouts, let's see what news they bring," said Jim.

"Well, what is it?" inquired Barnes, as the half-breed and two others came in from a scout. "Have you seen anything of them?"

"Yes," replied the half-breed; "he's just over there on the ridge, about two miles."

"Let's after them then, before they have time to get away," exclaimed Jim. "Perhaps in an hour or so they will be off again."

"Let's take two of the Indians with us," said Barnes. "If we find him and get the stone, it will be an easy matter for us to surprise the two Indians and lay them out."

"All right," replied Kingsbury. "Here, Frenchy, you and one of the others come with us, and we will go and capture them and get the 'stone', for I believe that the girl has got it with her."

"All right," said the half-breed, and he and the young chief, Strong Bear, followed the two assassins upon their villainous mission.

In the course of an hour, they had reached the ridge. Before them, and not a hundred yards away, stood the detective and Zell.

Pausing for a moment, to consider how to proceed, and, as they stood watching their victims, they saw, in the uplifted hand of the fair Zell, the unmistakeable gleam of the 'Great Medicine-stone'.

"Ah," muttered Barnes, "let me but get my fingers on that 'stone' again and all creation can't get it away from me again!"

Slowly, stealthily, cautiously, the two assassins crept up the hill toward their victims, leaving the two Indians behind. Closer and closer they crawled, till at last, they paused within twenty paces of their unsuspecting victims.

"Shoot him," whispered Kingsbury, quivering with excitement. "Don't give him a chance to escape.

Ah, see, he is examining the 'stone'.   No doubt he's gloating over the prospective wealth it will bring him. Steady, steady," continued Jim, as Barnes raised his rifle to a level with the broad shoulders of the detective. "For heaven's sake, don't miss him!"

"By thunder!" whispered Barnes, "I can't hold my gun steady.   Here, let me rest it over your shoulder. Still now."

And he laid the rifle over his companion's shoulder and, taking deliberate aim, fired.

—————:o:—————

THE GREAT MEDICINE STONE.

CHAPTER XXIII.

THE GREAT MEDICINE-STONE.

After leaving the cave, Charley and his companion hurried away as fast as they could toward the settlement. All day and till late into the night they toiled slowly on, stopping only occasionally to rest and to pick berries to eat.

"Here," said Charley, as they reached a high ridge, from which, in the day time, they could have seen the town of Hardscrabble, "here we will rest till morning. Lie down, Zell," he said, "and sleep. Here's a good bed beside this log; I can sit here and watch."

"No," said Zell, "I am not sleepy, I want to sit up a while. See, Charley, what I have got," she said, and she held the glittering diamond—'The Great Medicine-stone'—above her head, so that the moon-beams fell upon it and were reflected again in dazzling light. "See, do you know what it is, Charley?"

"It is either a diamond or a very good imitation of one," he answered, taking it from her hand and examining it closely. "Where did you get it, Zell?"

"My father bought it of some Indians about three or four weeks ago," she replied. "There is a long story connected with it. It is called 'The Great Medicine-stone', and was found in the Yukan River in Alaska. Did you ever hear of it?"

"Hear of it!" exclaimed Charley, as he looked back to his adventures of a few weeks ago and remembered again the sad story of the old hermit and of the twelve young men, who had given their lives in trying to possess it. "My God, Zell, I could tell stories of this

(171)

bloody gem, this 'Devil's Eye', that would freeze your
blood in your veins! But I don't believe the legend that
the Indians tell is true."

And he told her the story of the 'Great Medicine-
stone', as related by the old hermit.

''But then," he concluded, ''strange things do happen,
as I myself have seen; stranger even than fiction. See,"
he said, ''this 'stone' has twelve sides and each side is
named from one of the twelve months of the year," so
the legend says; ''and in the liquid depths of each face
is written or is reflected the destiny of him who reads or
looks upon it for that month. ''See," he laughed, as he
held the 'stone aloof; ''let us read our fate."

And laughingly he gazed upon the wonder-stone.

''My God!" he cried, as he looked upon the vision
that was revealed in the firy, liquid depths of the gem
—a vision which sent a chill of horror and dismay to
his brave heart; for, revealed there, were the figures of
two men, standing directly behind him, whom he recognized to be Kingsbury and Barnes. John Barnes
had just rested his rifle over the shoulder of his companion and was taking a steady and deliberate aim at
him. Quick as thought the detective saw and understood the revelation; for, like a polished mirror, the
'stone' reflected the scene and objects behind him.
He had seen the movement in raising the rifle and
could even see the triumphant faces of the assassins.
The bright, full moon shone full in the faces of the
men, so that he knew there could be no mistake.

Quick as lightning the detective dropped to the
ground, and at that very instant rang out loud and clear
upon the still night air the sharp report of the rifle.

With a wild, dispairing cry of horror and dismay, Zell sprang forward and knelt beside the fallen detective.

"Oh God," she wailed, "he is killed, he is killed! Charley, Charley," she called, "speak to me!"

"Ha, ha," cried Barnes, as he and Jim rushed upon the scene, "he will never speak again."

And he stooped to pick up the precious 'stone'. At the same time Kingsbury seized Zell's hand and in a tone of gloating triumph cried—

"Ah ha, my little beauty, I have got you again! Yes, yes, my darl—"

The words of insult which were crowding for utterance were cut short; for at that instant the gloating of the triumphant villains over their fallen enemy was changed into a scene of a very different nature.

The dead detective had in an instant, and very unexpectedly, come to life, and before the villains could realize what had happened, had sprung upon Kingsbury and dealt him a blow, which lay him bruised and bleeding at the feet of the girl, whom he had sought to destroy.

Turning then upon Barnes, the two men stood, for a moment, glaring upon each other. For an instant only they paused, then, like two wild and enraged beasts, they sprang upon each other and grappled in that fierce, desperate struggle which followed.

Swaying from side to side, reeling and staggering, they fought.

How the battle would have ended had they been left to fight it out unmolested, is hard to say. But they were not permitted to finish unmolested; for, Kingsbury, recovering from the stunning blow which he had received, had sufficiently recovered to realize the situation. Glad enough, indeed, would he have been to have left Barnes to fight it out alone, but he dared not; for his own life as well depended upon the issue of that battle.

Faint, dizzy, and so weak that he could not stand, he dragged himself upon his knees, shouting the while for the two Indians, whom they had left behind for fear that they might see the precious 'stone'; he drew his revolver, and watched for an opportunity to shoot the detective.

Scarcely ten feet away the two men fought. Now the detective was gaining the upper hand and, with crushing force, was bearing his opponent to the ground.

Kingsbury saw it, and with an awful fear at his heart, he raised his revolver and took aim. But here again an unexpected interference took place. For Zell, kneeling but a few feet away, praying for her friend, saw and understood the act. Quick as lightning, like an enraged lioness fighting for her mate, she sprang upon the unsuspecting wretch and, wrenching the revolver from his hand, dealt him a crushing blow upon his nose, which felled him bleeding and stunned at her feet.

"Ugh!" grunted the young Indian chief, who had arrived upon the scene. "Squaw-girl heap fight!"

"Help, help!" yelled Barnes, as the detective bore him to the ground.

The half-breed rushed to his assistance, and together, the two soon overpowered the already nearly exhausted detective and, in a moment, had him bound and helpless.

"Curse you!" cried John Barnes. "It powder and lead will kill you, you shall die!"

And drawing his revolver, he thrust its cold muzzle against the detective's temple and fired. But fate was against the villains; for, Zell had seen the act of the treacherous fiend, and striking at the hand which held the pistol, turned its muzzle from the detective's forehead to the heart of the villainous half-breed. Without a murmur, he fell lifeless at her feet.

With a fearful oath, Barnes raised the revolver again; but here he was stopped again. For the young Indian sprang forward and seized the revolver and, wrenching it from the murderer's hand, said in a low, stern tone—

"No kill, take him back to village with us!"

"Stand back, red man!" hissed Barnes threatingly. "Don't interfere with me!"

"Ugh! me no afraid!" he said, and his hand rested upon the hilt of his hunting knife. "Take him back to village."

"All right!" said Barnes; and there was a dangerous light in his wicked eyes. "We will take him back."

In the course of an hour, the two prisoners, with hands tied behind them, and tied together, for Zell was no longer considered harmless, were marched away.

But they did not return to the Indian camp. The village was nearly in an opposite direction, so they started directly for the village. For two hours they marched on, and then went into camp.

On the march, Charley had found time to talk to his companion; and, to cheer her up and to pass away time, he told her of how he first found the clue which led him to their retreat.

"And who is this lady friend of yours?" asked Zell.

"Oh," said Charley, "I didn't think you would be much interested in her, but I thought you would be interested in him."

"Indeed I am interested in him," she answered, "but, perhaps not as you think."

"He gave me the best of reasons for supposing as I do," said Charley.

"I don't understand what those reasons can be," replied Zell.

"Neither do I, unless love can be taken as a reason."

"He certainly had no right to talk of love between us. He was a friend, no more; and as a friend, I am interested in his welfare. But your lady friend, I want to hear of her; what is her name? Of course it's no one I know."

"Yes it is."

"Oh Charley!" cried Zell, "please tell me who it is!"

"It is your cousin, Kitty Barnes."

"Cousin Kitty! For heaven's sake, has she come here?" cried Zell.

"She came with John."

"Where is she staying?"

"She is with Frank. I left her there to take care of him," said Charley.

"Ah! well, Frank and Kitty will get along all right. She will just suit him and, I think, that he will suit her pretty well, too. That is if she—she—"

"Well, 'if she' what?" iuterrupted Charley.

But Zell did not hear, or at least, appeared not to.

"Zell," said Charley, after a short pause, "do you know that that man there," pointing to Barnes, "is Kitty's brother?"

"No, no! O don't tell me that!" she exlaimed, looking up into Charley's face with an incredulous look in her beautiful blue eyes.

"But he is, Zell, and he helped to kill your father— his uncle; and all for that cursed diamond. Oh, how I wish that you had killed Jim that day in the cave, or had let me kill him. It would have saved all this trouble, Zell."

"Oh, I could not do it, Charley; he used to be a friend of mine. I could not bear to see *you* kill him," she said; and there was a peculiar emphasis upon the "you".

"You came pretty near killing him last night, or to-night, rather. By jingoes, but he's got a bad looking face on him now, sure!"

"Oh, I could have killed him then!"

"Zell," said Charley, as they went into camp, "there's something up. Jim and John are plotting mischief; I believe that they mean to kill that Indian, so they will have everything to themselves."

"They are afraid of him. Do you know, Charley, he is the Fawn's lover?"

"Ah, then that is why he interfered and prevented Barnes from killing me; he did it for your sake, Zell. They mean to lay him out, but I don't know how we can help him."

"We must manage to warn him," said Zell. "If I can get to speak to him."

CHAPTER XXIX.

FREE.

"Wait and watch. Just a word will be sufficient."

A half hour after going into camp, the Indian came along where Charley and Zell sat. They were bound to a tree in a position so that Zell could lie down. For a moment the Indian stood silently, looking upon the fair young girl with a dark frown upon his brow, but he said nothing. Here was a chance, and Zell whispered but a word or two of warning. He uttered not a word in response, but in his dark eye there blazed a light of unmistakable fire which told plainer than words could have told, that he heard and understood. For a long time they sat and talked; but at last Zell lay down and was soon asleep in spite of her deplorable condition. Midnight had long since passed and the moon had gone down, leaving them in total darkness. The detective was awake and thinking of the strange conduct of the Indian brave and wondering what the result would be, for he knew that the two white renegades were planning vengeance against him for interfering, when he felt the rope which bound his hands, slacken, and a moment later, a huge hunting knife dropped into his lap. With an inexpressible feeling of joy he found his hands free. It was but the work of an instant to sever the bonds which bound his feet as well as those which bound his sleeping companion.

"Zell, he whispered, after listening for a moment to assure himself that all was well, "come, wake up, we are free; let's be off."

In silence they crept away. Out into the dark,

THE DEATH OF JOHN BARNES.

gloomy forest and to liberty. Oh! what a feeling of joy and thankfulness filled their hearts as they found themselves once more free.

They had reached the margin of a dark and dismal swamp and were hurrying along its edge, when they were startled by the report of a pistol shot, which came from the direction of the spot they had just left.

"What can it mean, I wonder?" asked Zell, while her heart throbbed with fear.

"Perhaps they have discovered our escape; but I don't know what the shot means, unless they have shot the Indian," replied Charley. "I believe that they intended to kill him. Once rid of him, they could easily dispose of me; then Kingsbury would have no one to interfere with his satisfying his fiendish ambition."

"Oh my God!" murmured Zell, as she thought of the fate that would have been hers. "Oh, how thankful I ought to be to you for the noble friendship you have shown me. Oh, I thank God for such a noble friend!"

"Tut, tut, Zell," said Charley, "I am doing nothing more than any young fellow would do for such a pretty girl as you are."

"Oh, I don't like your flattery, Charley, nor are your words true, for here are two young men, both of whom have had the same opportunity which you have had, but they have not done it. Oh Charley, when I think of this, of the suffering and danger that you have endured for me—a poor, friendless girl—I can't help but to show my feeling of gratitude!"

"Well, well, girls are apt to be sentimental sometimes," he said; "but come, you are about ready to drop down from exhaustion; let's stop here and rest

till morning.   No one will find us here in this dismal
swamp.   Lie down and sleep."

"Oh, I am so tired," she moaned, "I could almost
wish I were dead."

"Don't get discouraged, Zell; we will stay here till
morning.   We will be safe here and a good nap will
make you feel like a new girl.   Lie down and sleep;
I will watch."

So tired and worn, poor Zell was asleep almost as
soon as her head touched its pillow upon the detective's lap.

For some time Charley sat, leaning back against a
tree and thinking.   But soon he, too, slept.

Morning came.   The warm, bright sun was climbing
slowly above the mountain peaks, awakening the birds
to song and gladness; still the girl slept on, though the
detective had awakened.

Oh what a vision of loveliness!" he mused! as he
gazed long and earnestly upon that slight, graceful
form lying there with her golden head pillowed upon his
knees.   "What a sweet, beautiful face!" Long and wist-
fully he gazed upon the beautiful vision.   But we will
not commit the folly of telling the thoughts which filled
his heart—thoughts that had never found place there
before.   The vision of that happy home, those bright-
eyed, laughing children, and, last but not least, the
beautiful, girlish wife who greeted him with a loving
kiss, which he had seen in his dream.   Ah, it was this
same sweet face which he saw; there was the same glad,
happy smile.

"Oh God!" murmured Charley, "can I hope for such
happiness?"

But here his musings were brought to an end, for, out upon the still morning air rang out loud and distinct the report of a pistol shot, followed by a cry of pain and terror. Again all was still. The shot that had caused that cry was not far away and it came so clear and distinct, that he almost thought he recognized from whose lips it came.

With a start Zell awakened and looked wildly about her as if expecting every moment to see their enemies rush upon them from the deep shadows of the swamp.

"Listen; Zell," said the detective, "I can hear some one talking." Listening they could plainly hear some one talking.

"Curse you, John Barnes," came in the voice of Jim Kingsbury, "die like a miserable dog that you are! The 'stone' is mine now—all mine; and I will yet have the girl too! There's a band of horse thieves not far from here and I will go there; I can get all the help I want from them. Yes, I will go there; so fare you well, my friend; I hope that you may die easy and may the devil have a fire ready for your reception.

"Look!" he cried, holding the precious gem before the dying man's eyes; "Ha, ha; I picked it up while you and the detective were fighting. I saw where he dropped it when you shot at him. Oh, isn't it a beauty? It's worth a clean half million. Ha, ha, and it's all mine!"

"I will go to the outlaws' camp and stay there till I am well; then I will follow after the girl. Ho, but I will have her yet! Well, John, I will have to leave you; sorry, but I cant help it—can't possibly, my dear friend; for I must reach the outlaws' camp before that cursed

Indian returns with help.   Curse you anyway for missing him; why couldn't you have made a better shot?
you only broke his arm.   He and his whole tribe will be
after us before long."

"Curse you, Jim Kingsbury!" came in a feeble voice
from Barnes, as Jim turned and left the dying man alone.
"Curse you, you treacherous villain, and may vengeance
overtake you!"

"Zell," said Charley, "John Barnes is your cousin, as
bad as he is, let us go and find him."

"O Charley!" cried Zell, "is it possible that that man
is my cousin?"

"Yes, Zell," replied Charley, as he forced his way
through the swamp that hid him from them.

In a few minutes they came upon him as he lay with
his head resting upon his hand and his feet in the water
where he had fallen when shot down by his treacherous
companion.

With a shudder he met the pitying, forgiving eyes of
Zell, and there was a wild look in his terror-stricken
face.   Then, with a wild shriek of terror he closed his
eyes, and in a moment was dead.

"Come, Zell," said the detective, "we can't do anything for him.   Come, let us go,"and he took her hand
and led her away from the horrible scene.

For miles they tramped on through the mountains,
and at night, closely wrapping his coat about his companion bade her lie down and rest.   Tired and hungry,
the poor girl curled herself up beside a fallen tree and
was soon asleep.   Charley, seating himself beside her,
sat watching and thinking for hours.   But at last he,
too, slept.

Long after midnight, the two fugitives were aroused from their dreams by the discharge of firearms, followed by a wild chorus of yells and shouts. For half an hour the battle in the darkness lasted; then all was still again. The battle had been won.

"What can it mean, Charley?" asked Zell, nervously.

"I don't know," he answered, "but I am glad that we are not there. Perhaps the Indians have followed Kingsbury to the outlaws' camp that he spoke of and have attacked them. He said that they were not far away. Well, they are no friends of ours anyway, so we will not bother ourselves about them,"

"Let's go away from here, Charley, I can't sleep any more, and I am rested now," said Zell, fearing that some of the Indians or outlaws might come that way.

"Well, I guess perhaps that we had better," said Charley. ' "Here, take my arm and let me help you." Thus they tramped on through the woods and mountains till, a little after sunrise, they stood upon the summit of a high ridge from whence, away to the North, they could see the town of Hardscrabble.

"O Look, look!" cried Zell, clapping her hands in delight. "O Charley, it is a town!"

"Yes," said Charley, "it is the town of Hardscrabble. That is where I started from when I set out to find the old hermit and his beautiful daughter—"

"For shame, Charley!" said Zell, blushing crimson at his thoughtless words.

"I beg your pardon, Zell, I didn't mean anything," he said, "but I can't take it back for it is the truth. But then, of course, I ought not to have said it all the same. If it was Kitty now, instead of you, I could call her pretty without fear of offending."

"O Charley, I am not offended, indeed I am not."

CHAPTER XXX.

"Oh," said the detective, "I didn't think you were very, very much offended; but see, Zell, it is nearly twenty miles from here to the settlement; do you think that you can walk that far?"

"Yes." replied Zell, bravely; "I can walk there all right, if I can get a little something to eat. Oh, I am nearly starved!"

"We will have some breakfast before long," said Charley, encouragingly.

"But I don't see how we are to get it," said Zell, dubiously.

"I will show," said Charley. "See that little stream down there?" and he pointed to a small stream which ran through the valley below. "Well, there's fish in there and I have got a hook and line in my jacket; do you see now?"

"Oh, yes," she answered, "I see; but let's hurry; I am anxious to be eating some of them."

A half hour later they stopped and kindled a fire upon the bank of the stream and, while Charley caught a few delicious mountain trout, Zell prepared their breakfast by roasting the fish, Indian fashion, by holding them before the fire stuck upon the end of little sticks. A dozen or more were thus prepared, when Zell declared that she could wait no longer; so they sat down and partook of their hastily prepared meal.

(184)

CHARLEY AND ZELL ON THEIR WAY DOWN THE RIVER.

"O, how delicious," cried the hungry girl.

"They lack a little salt, that's all," declared the detective.

"Well," declared Zell, after satisfying her hunger, "I feel better now; and I am ready to march."

"We will rest awhile first," said Charley, stretching himself at full length upon the grassy bank. For some time he lay watching the sweet face of his little companion who, sitting but a little way off, was busying herself with pinning up the rips and tares in her clothes.

"Pretty near an endless task, ain't it, Zell?" he asked.

"Yes," she answered, "but I hate to be seen so ragged."

"Where did you get your pins?"

"Oh," she laughed, "I got them off of that thorn bush there."

"Ah, that's something you have learned from the Indians, I suppose."

"Charley," said Zell, as she finished her task, "do you think that there's any danger of my being arrested when I get to town?"

"Arrested! Thunder, no!" he cried. "No one will arrest you unless I take a notion to."

"I didn't know, I just wanted to know what you thought about it. Well, I am ready to go now."

"All right; will march on then. I don't think that we will have to walk more than five or six miles before we will find a ranch. We will follow down the river," he said, and they set out on their journey.

Some five miles below, they came to on old hunter's camp und stopped to rest and eat the first meal of bread, butter, potatoes and coffee, with a few other things that they had sat down to since the evening that they left the little cabin and set out to search for the hermit.

The old man had a small canoe which he loaned them and, in a few minutes after finishing their dinner, they started down the river for town.

At a little after sunset, they arrived at Hardscrabble, and a few minutes later they arrived at the hotel where Frank Smith and Kitty Barnes met them and welcomed them back to the land of the living.

Kitty soon marched her cousin off to her own room where, of course, we have no right to intrude.

A half hour after, when their supper was announced, Charley was not only surprised but was puzzled at the appearance of the two girls. For, on entering the room where Charley and Frank were waiting, the two cousins looked so much alike that, for a few minutes, neither Charley nor Frank could see which was which.

"By ginger," declared Charley, "which is which anyway?" Ah, I know, I can see the mischief in your eye, Miss Kitty. This is Zell. Come, let's go to supper."

Three days after this, the detective set out on his search for Kingsbury. He had sworn, as we have seen, to avenge the death of Zell's father and, with this object in view, he began his work.

For two weeks he searched and finally found a clew to the whereabouts of the murderer.

"I don't know for sure," he said, one evening as he was talking with Zell about his work; "I can't say yet whether I have found him or not, but I believe that I have. I think that he is down at deep canyon mines' some forty miles northwest of here. I am going down there again to-morrow."

"I wish that I could help you, Charley," said Zell; "It's too bad for you to go alone."

"Oh, I don't mind, so that I know that you are safe," replied Charley.

"Oh, I wish I could only know that you were safe too!" said the blushing girl. "Oh, here comes Kitty!"

"Oh, you rogue!" cried Kitty, "what means these blushes?" But Zell was gone.

———:o:———

CHAHTER XXXI.

One evening about three weeks after the arrival of Charley and Zell at Hardscrabble, Kitty came bounding into the sitting-room, and clasping her hands in glee, she cried—

"Oh Zell! arn't it jolly though? There's to be a grand ball at the Marshe's! It's to be the grandest affair of the season! Come, cheer up; don't look so glum! Arn't Charley home yet?"

"No," replied Zell, "I think not."

"Think not! just as though you wouldn't know! But then it don't matter so very much; for, there's Albert Dumars, all the girls in town are just crazy after him. Oh, he's almost too elegant for anything—you will let him take you, won't you, Zell dear?"

"No, I won't; so there!"

"Phew, Miss pert! So you will let that Lucy King walk off with the prize, will you? I just wouldn't do it. I don't care if you don't want him."

"Oh Kitty, for shame to talk so! What would Charley say? What would he think of me?" cried Zell reproachfully.

Just then, Frank Smith and Albert Dumars entered the room. A word in regard to Dumars will suffice for now, as he will play a very prominent part in this story henceforth. He was a young man of twenty-six years

(188)

At the Ball.

of age; a very handsome, dashing, and superbly elegant in dress and manner; attractively winning and, as Kitty has said, was considered a prize. As they entered the room, Kitty greeted them with the exclamation:

"Oh, you bad boys; you are always happening around just when you are being talked about."

"Ah, and so you were talking about us, were you, Miss Zell?" said Dumars with his latest and most elegant bow, approaching Zell, as Kitty had appropriated Frank for herself—as she had a right to do, for it was whispered that they were already engaged—leaving Dumars to the tender mercy of the charming Zell. "Speak of the absent, and they will be sure to surprise you by their appearance," he said.

"Oh, I wish it were true!" exclaimed Zell, quickly.

"Ah!" murmured Dumars, with a significant shrug of the shoulders. But come to the piano, Miss Zell, I have not heard you sing for so long; please favor us with your favorite."

Seating herself at the piano, Zell sang in her sweet, clear voice: "My Rover Will Come Again."

Several young people had entered the room and gathered around to hear her. She sang, as it seemed to those gathered about her, as she had never sang before— as though her whole heart and soul were wrapped up in the thought which those words inspired—that her "Rover would come again."

"Oh Zell," cried Kitty; then bending over her, she whispered: "Don't, Zell, please don't do it again. Dumars is vanished—poor fellow! Come now," she said, "let's go and put on our raps, it's time to go. The guest's are already gathering.

Already, the sweet strains of music came floating out upon the quiet evening air, bidding our friends and their guests to come. Putting on their wraps, they were ready and Kitty said, pleadingly:

"Just this once Zell, Charley won't care, I know he won't !"

"No," said Zell, "I won't do it! He knows very well that I don't want his company; I will certainly refuse him if he asks me—let him go with those that want his company."

"Come then," said Kitty, taking her cousin's arm and marching her off; "I won't give him a chance to ask you. He and Frank can amuse themselves with the other girls if they want to."

"It's too bad to drop Frank," said Zell.

"Oh, it will be all right with him, he will understand what it means," answered Kitty, as they set out together.

Down through the elegant parlors of the Marsh mansion, as they entered, floated the sweet strains of the waltz. The gay throngs of dancers were flitting about or gayly chatting in little groups and pairs. Each fair maiden had her especial group of admirers; but in all that gay throng of charming damsels, there was not one so ardently sought for or so much admired as was the fair and charming Zell.

"O Zell," cried Kitty, gayly, "isn't this jolly? But here comes the dashing Dumars, he is just dying to win your favor. Did you see him dancing with Lucy? Ah, but she's—"

"O don't, Kitty!" remonstrated Zell, as she saw Dumars approaching.

"Ah, Miss Zell, may I have the pleasure of your company for this charming waltz?" asked Dumars.

"It is my favorite and you, better than any one else. can assist me."

"Thank you," said Zell demurely, accepting his invitation. And together, they went whirling down through the brilliantly lighted parlors, the pride or envy, as the case suited of all that vast throng.

Supper was announced, and Frank and Kitty, Dumars and Zell went down together.

After supper, Zell and Kitty were seated with their friends, chatting with one another, when Dumars approached and in his bland, smooth tone asked:

"It is my right, I believe, Miss Zell, to claim this dance with you: may I have the honor?"

"O, Zell," cried Kitty, bursting tempestuously, as was her want, upon the scene, "here comes Charley! Oh, Mr. Dumars, are you acquainted with our mentor? Let me introduce you, Mr. Dumars, let me acquaint you with my friend, Mr. Shipton."

"Happy to meet you, Mr. Shipton. My lady friends here have often spoken to me of you."

Zell raised her eyes with a look of surprise at this statement of Mr. Dumars, for she well knew that neither she nor Kitty had done anything of the kind.

"It is a pleasure, I assure you, to meet any one of the young ladies' friends," said Charley. "And now, Miss Kitty, how do you do?" he inquired, taking her outstretched hand. "You look quite happy and I guess that you are enjoying yourself well enough with Frank, so I will leave you to take care of yourselves for the present. And now," said Charley, turning to Zell.

"Excuse me, Mr. Dumars," said Zell.

"Ah, certainly," he said politely, and with a graceful bow, he turned and joined Frank and Kitty.

"How is my little friend, Zell?" asked the detective. "You look tired, you have been dancing too much, I fear."

"Oh, I am tired, Charley," she said, "but not with dancing, for I have danced but very little. But you, Charley, how have you fared?"

"Tolerably well, Zell; that's all one could expect of me."

"Where have you been?" she asked.

"Down to Deep Canon mines; but then, I won't tell you now. You were engaged for this dance to Dumars; don't disapoint him, Zell; I can wait.

"No, no, I don't want to dance, I want you to tell me the news. You have been away four days—it seems a month to me—you are away nearly all the time. But have you learned anything, Charley, for sure, yet, about Kingsbury?"

"Yes, I have trailed him to his hiding place. He is down there."

"Come in here, Charley," said Zell, leading him into a conservatory; "we will be alone in here; no one will hear us. Now tell me all about where you have been."

"Ah, Zell," said Charley, taking both her little hands in his broad, brown palms, and looking down into her dark blue eyes, with such a longing, wistful look, "I was down to your old home. I went to the Indian village and learned that that band of horse thieves that Kingsbury spoke of had been broken up. The Indians surprised them that night after John was killed. That was the battle we heard that night. I trailed those that escaped to Deep Canon. Jim was one of the lucky ones. But his day is coming soon. I could have arrested him, but there are more of them and they are up to some new game and I want to find out what it is and get the rest of the gang. There's some devilish plot or game on hand and this Dumars has a hand in it, that is why I came back so soon; I want to see what he is up to."

"O, Charley, how I wish that I could help you; I am sick and tired of all this. Nothing but one continual round of gayety, flattery and nonsense. It just suits Kitty, but I don't like it—it makes me tired. Oh, it is refreshing, indeed, to have one good, true hearted friend than one can go to after all this!"

"Ah, Zell," he murmured, standing before her and holding both her hands in his, while he read, in her beautiful eyes gazing so trustfully, so lovingly into his own, the love of a pure young heart; "you ought to be happy, if beauty and a host of admiring friends could make a girl happy."

But the grand ball was over. Tired and weary; many with aching heads and some, perhaps, with aching hearts, the guests turned their faces homeward.

————:o:————

CHAPTER XXXII.

"I say, Kingsbury, how—"

"Confound your imprudence, you idiot, if you ever call me by that name again, I'll be the death of you!" cried Kingsbury, alias King, angrily.

"Ah, beg pardon, Mr. King," said Dumars, I forgot!"

"It won't be healthy for you if you forget again!" declared Kingsbury. But what is the news? How's things up at Hardscrabble? You were there last night, were you not?"

"Yes, I was there last night and there was a grand ball at the Marshe's and, of course, all the big bugs were out. I saw young Smith and Kitty Barnes and had the honor of dancing with Miss Zell."

"You are too infernal familiar with Zell, Albert Dumars, but what about that devilish detective, did you see anything of him?"

"See him! I should smile; and I had an introduction to him too," replied Dumars.

"Ah! then you were certainly able to learn something of what he is doing."

"Not much! I have put in two weeks of faithful work—I have worked Frank and Kitty, but I couldn't do anything with Zell."

"And how about Lucy, has she learned anything?" asked King.

(194)

THE DARK FIGURE.

"No."

"Well, what is Charley doing anyway, did you find out?"

"No, I could'nt find out. He has been away for the last four or five days, but I couldn't find out where he had gone. I didn't get to see him till last night, at the dance, just after supper. I took Zell to supper and was to dance with her, when Charley came along and took her away from me."

"You say that he has been there for four or five days till last night?"

"Yes."

"Dumars, I will tell you what it is, that cunning devil is on our track! Something must be done, and there is no time to dally about it either. What have you learned anyway that will give us a clue as to what he is up to?"

"Not a solitary thing about him. But I learned one thing that I believe will help us out: Kitty and Frank are going to get married soon and then they will go to Helena. I think that they calculate to stay there. Of course, Zell will go with them, and so will Charley."

"Good! That suits me very well. I will just drop a card to Dick Taylor and have him prepare a reception for them. Ah, there's nothing like having everything arranged beforehand."

"I will tell you my plan, Jim," said Dumars. "This thing is sure to come off in a few days: they will be married before a week at most. We can do nothing more here, and I believe that Charley has been down about our old camping ground to see if he couldn't find out something; perhaps he has even traced us here. Those devilish Indians will give us away for they have, ever since that night that you laid Barnes out—"

"Course you, Dumars," cried King, in a rage, "don't you ever mention that affair again! But go on with your plans; let us see what they are."

"Well, it is this: You go on to Helena and arrange things with Dick, and I will stay here and make arrangements to go with them; and I can let you know of any change in their plans if there are any, you know."

"All right!" replied Kingsbury.

"And now, where are the boys?" asked Dumars.

"Jack and Dick are down to the dance hall, of course. Are you sure, Dumars, that those two fellows are all right?"

"Yes, they are all right; we can trust them, never you fear about that. And now, I must have a little rest, for I must be back to Hardscrabble to-morrow evening; as I have an engagement there that I must keep without fail."

"Ah, well," mused Jim, as he found himself alone; "all is playing into my hands again and I can well afford to wait for a while yet. I have rid myself of all but that devilish detective, and I will do him up one of these fine days, 'and then, my pretty little Zell, you shall complete what the diamond lacks, of making me rich and happy. A clean half million and a beautiful wife, then I'll away to some foreign land where I can enjoy myself for the rest of my days in peace and plenty. Ah, Zell, my little beauty, I will soon prepare a cage for you! Yes, I will go on before and prepare a welcome for you and for h i m," said Kingsbury, and ringing for a waiter, he called for writing materials.

"Ah, John," he said, as the waiter (a Chinaman), brought the desired articles, "has any new comers arrived to-dav?"

"Yes; one lady and one man."

"How did they come, John?" he asked.

"On, stage from Gallatin," replied John.

"No others, John?" he asked, as he placed a shining quarter in the Celestials hand.

"No, no more."

"All right; that's all," he said, "and now, to arrange things. I have a little game of my own; I don't just know about that Dumars; I don't like his style; I won't trust him anyway. I will send a letter to Dick Taylor to have the boys at the "Pass"; and then I will go up just before they do. I can depend on Dick; he will do up the detective and Dumars too, then the coast will be clear."

Taking up the pen, he wrote long and carefully. Finally, he threw down the pen and, with a gleam of triumph in his eyes, he muttered:

"There! that settles it, Dick Taylor and his gang of desperadoes will attend to the rest, Dumars included."

For some time, he sat in silence deeply absorbed in thought; when, suddenly, as if awaking from some horrible dream, he sprang to his feet and looking wildly about, he muttered:

"God, but I must have something to drink, something to drive away this horrible night mare! Oh, the image of that old man's face! I can see him now, as he fell— O curse you, James Barnes; can't you rest in your grave in peace!"

"In my grave! Ha, ha!" came in a low, hissing

whisper, which to the horrified man seemed to be directly at his side.

Springing to his feet, Jim rushed franticly from the room and down the stairs to the barroom and called for whiskey. In his terror and excitement, forgetting all else save to banish the horrifying image of the murdered man's face from his mind.

Scarcely had he left the room, when a dark figure glided quickly and silently to the table. For a few minutes, the figure bent over the telltale letter, scanning its contents closely; and then, as footsteps sounded in the hall below, the figure glided as swiftly and silently away again.

"It's all right," muttered Kingsbury, as he entered the room and picked up the letter, "but curse my imprudence for leaving it there! No preying eyes have seen it, but it was risky business just the same."

Folding the letter, he placed it in an inside pocket and then retired for the night. But it was long before sleep came to his guilty conscience. Visions of the past few weeks rushed through his mind in such vivid and awful distinctness as to nearly drive him frantic. But, finally, under the influence of the liquor which he had drunk, he dozed off with a drunken stupor, rather than sleep. But even in this condition, horrible dreams haunted him and made life almost intolerable.

———:o:———

DUMARS AND LUCY.

CHAPTER XXXIII.

LUCY.

Early the next morning, Kingsbury arose from the couch where he had passed a night of misery and horror. Worn and weary, he dropped himself down to the stage office and mailed his letter to the outlaw chief.

"Now," he muttered, "I will go up to Hardscrabble and see what Dumars is a doing. I must see Lucy before I go. She must manage to go up to Helena with Zell. I will arrange things with her, for I can't trust Dumars. I wonder what he is a doing anyway—nothing good, I'll venture. I'll just drop in on them to-night and see what he's up to with her, and then before morning I will be off; for it will never do for me to be caught here in daylight."

As the Deep Canon stage drew up before the Wayfarers hotel at Hardscrabble that evening, Jim Kingsbury, alias King, stepped from the stage and stood upon the porch before the tavern. As he stood there, Lucy King (his sister) and Dumars came out of the hotel and for a moment stood before him. So well was he disguised, that they did not recognize him in the guise of the rough miner, the accomplice and brother.

"I wonder who that rough-looking fellow was?" queried Lucy. "He looked at me as if he knew me or would like to eat me."

(199)

"No, no, Lucy dear, not like to eat you, but never mind, you know; beauty is attractive to all, whatever and by whomever seen. But come, remember our engagement; let us hasten on, for it is getting late."

"O Albert," murmured Lucy.

*   *   *   *   *

"Who is it?" queried the speaker's companion, in a sad, pitying tone, drooping her head.

"He is Albert Dumars."

"And she."

"Is Lucy King," he answered. And, in silence, they passed on and disappeared in the darkness.

But why not have drawn the curtain of delicacy here and shut this picture from view, some may ask? Ah, I will tell you: In the first place, this dishonorable act was but the laying of that foundation upon which was to be enacted a scene which forms one of the principal features of this life sketch. Again, it is a true picture of Western life as we find it. Why, then seek to conceal the darker shades of life, revealing only the bright and beautiful?

Censure me who will! A picture of life, like that of a landscape, would be incomplete without the dark shadows that mark the places where the bright sunshine stops.

"Confound it anyway," muttered Kingsbury, as he watched the two disappearing forms; "where are they going anyway, I wonder!" I must see her and it won't do for me to stay here till morning. I wonder if I can overtake them? If I only knew where they were going," he mused, and he set out down the street.

"Ah, the Eldorado," he mused, as he stopped before

the dance hall. "I wonder if they would—but no, Dumars would dare not bring her here; no, no; besides, she wouldn't go to such a place. No doubt they are at some place of amusement and won't be back till late.

Suddenly, and as though some new and happy thought had burst upon his troubled mind, he turned a corner and walked rapidly down another street. A few blocks farther on, and under the full glare of a street lamp he came suddenly upon Zell and Kitty who had just met at the postoffice where Charley and Frank had stopped to enquire for letters while the two girls walked slowly on.

With a subdued exclamation of surprise and admiration at the beautiful vision before him, Kingsbury checked his hurried steps for a moment; but, seeing the approach of the two men who had just left the postoffice door, and whom he recognized to be Charley and Frank, he hurried on again.

"Go on, my pretty bird," he muttered, "but the day is soon coming when I'll cage you!" And hurrying on down the street, he soon found himself knocking at a door.

"Here," he mused, "for an hour or two, under the influence of wine, can I find a respite from this horrible nightmare which haunts me night and day."

Then, by a chance, or otherwise, as the case may be, he found himself beneath the same roof which sheltered his sister, for whom he was searching, but whom he did not expect to find there.

————:o:————

CHAPTER XXXIV.

A WEDDING.

"O Kitty," cried Zell, as she gave a quick, frightened glance behind her, at the retreating form of Kingsbury in the guise of a rough miner, "did you see that man? Did you notice anything strange about him?"

"Why no!" laughed Kitty, "I didn't notice him at all. You are always seeing strange looks and actions in every rough man that you meet; but then, I don't wonder much that you do!"

"O why don't the boys come? I could get all the letters in the postoffice in less time!" cried Zell.

"O fie, Zell; don't be frightened! Here they come now. Oh, you had better be coming!" she exclaimed, taking Frank's arm and walking on in advance.

"What's the matter, Zell?" asked the detective, as he drew her arm through his and looked down in her frightened axious face.

"O Charley," she exclaimed excitedly, "I have seen Jim Kingbury; we just passed him as we turned the corner by the postoffice. Didn't you see him, Charley?"

"No, Zell, I didn't; or, at least, I didn't recognize him."

"He was disguised as a miner."

"Perhaps you were mistaken, Zell."

"No, no, I was not mistaken; he looked surprised when he saw me and he muttered something; I couldn't hear what!" cried Zell.

KITTY AND ZELL.

"Well, let him go for the present; we will have a reckoning with him some day and, perhaps, before long."

"Did you get me a letter, Charley?" asked Zell.

"Yes, Zell, I have a letter for you. It is from Helena. Do you know any one there?" he asked, handing her the letter.

"No, I don't know of any one there that I know. O Charley," she exclaimed, scrutinizing the writing, "I do believe that it is my brother Fred's writing!"

"But how can he know about your being here?"

"I wrote to my sister Kate, when I first came here, and she has written to him, I suppose. Let's hurry home and see what he has to say." said Zell, as she placed the letter in her pocket and hurried on.

"Kitty, look, look!" cried Zell, as she and her companion reached their boarding house. "Oh, I have got a letter, see? It's from Fred!" And breaking the seal, she read it to her friends.

It was her brother who was at Helena. He was interested in a rich mining property at the new mines of Ceur-De-Lion and wanted her, her friend and Frank and Kitty to come on and go there with him.

"Kate is coming soon," he wrote, "and then, if you come, we will be together again. I suppose that Frank and Kitty are married by this time * * * Come as soon as possible, for I want to reach the mines in time to prepare for winter."

Oh, won't that be jolly!" cried Kitty, clapping her hands in glee. Oh Charley, you will go; Zell can't go without you, can you, Zell?"

"I guess that he will go with us," said the girl blushing crimson at her cousin's frankness.

"Yes, I will go too," said Charley.   "I have got business as far as Helena, anyway."

So it was arranged.   They were to start just as soon as possible.

"I want to arrest Kingsbury before we leave here," said the detective, "but I am not ready yet."

And so the time passed quickly.   But the detective was not idle, for he had shadowed Kingsbury till, at last, becoming alarmed, he had fled upon the very day when the detective was going to arrest him.

Two weeks had passed since Zell had received her letter; it was Kitty's wedding day.   All Hardscrabble felt called upon to celebrate the grand event.   A grand ball was on the programme, and everything was ready; everybody was happy.

"Charley," said Zell, meeting the detective as he returned from his fruitless search for Kingsbury, radiant with smiles and blushes; "do you not enjoy this? You look troubled, disappointed; is there anything wrong?" she asked anxiously.

"No, nothing that need to worry anyone.   I didn't find Kingsbury; he has fled; he has friends here that have found out in some way that I was 'going to arrest him and they have warned him."

"Is that all, Charley?" she asked, with a sigh of relief.

"Yes; but where are Frank and Kitty, Zell?" he asked.

"Oh, they are down in the parlor, entertaining their friends and receiving congratulations.   We were disappointed, Charley, because you were not here."

"I couldn't help it, Zell. I wanted to be here, for I never saw anyone get married," he answered.

"Oh," murmured Zell, "you ought to have been here. But it is time to go to the ball. I suppose we will have to go, Charley, but I don't want to," she said, as she excused herself and left him to finish her toilet. In a few minutes she returned and announced that she was ready.

"Ah, Zell," said Charley admiringly, "you are a pretty girl!"

"For shame, Charley," she exclaimed, turning her blushing face away from him; "how long since have you turned flatterer?"

Oh, I mean your clothes are pretty, Zell; I didn't mean you, for that word wouldn't come anywhere near expressing my opinion of you," he declared. "But where are the old folks?"

"The old folks! what do you mean?"

"Kitty and Frank, of course. They are old folks now; at least I should feel old if I were married. And there was a sly twinkle in his honest, gray eyes.

"Oh, they have gone. Come let's go, we will be late," she said.

"Oh, I didn't think that you were in a hurry; but come, let's be off."

"I ain't in a hurry, Charley, please don't think that of me; I would rather not go at all, for I know you don't want to go. But tell me, Charley, what is it that troubles you—I know there's something besides what you said about Jim. It isn't fair to keep anything from me."

"Oh, I have caught onto a little game lately that worries me a little. Jim Kingsbury knows about our going to Helena—Dumars and Lucy have told him, I suppose—and he has made arrangements to meet us on the road. Of course, Zell, you know what his object is. It's the thought of what might have happened, had I not learned of their plans. He has made arrangements with Dick Taylor and his gang of desperados and horsethieves that infest the vicinity of Helena, to meet us at the 'Pass'. I don't know what or where the 'Pass' is, but of course, we can avoid them. "Have you seen Lucy and Dumars to-day to speak with them?" asked Charley.

"No," replied Zell, "I have not, nor do I want to see them."

"They intend to go with us, I believe," said Charley.

"Oh, I hope not," said Zell.

"Dumars and Kingsbury are working together; Lucy has a hand in it too, or, at least, they use her. Did you know that Jim had a sister?"

"No," replied Zell, "I didn't know any of his folks; I never heard of his sister. Is Lucy his sister?"

"Yes, Lucy is his sister. He goes by the name of King here," said Charley.

"Ah, we are late," said Zell, as they entered the hall, "and here comes Kitty."

"Oh you naughty girl," exclaimed Kitty, "what have you been doing so long? Come and take off your wraps—"

"Let me congratulate you first, Kitty; Mrs. Smith, I should have said," said Charley, seizing her hand and giving it a squeeze that brought the tears into her sparkling eyes.

"Oh!" she cried. "Thank you, Charley, I will return the congratulation before long, I think. "Dear!" exclaimed Kitty, as they returned to the hall, "what a rough boy he is! He nearly broke my fingers."

"Ah, Miss Zell," said Dumars, as they came into the hall, "may I have the pleasure of your company for this dance?"

"Excuse me, Mr. Dumars," replied Zell, with a blush of shame upon her cheeks, as she turned and walked away.

"By ginger," exclaimed Charley a few hours later, as they were returning home, "you did it nicely. Zell!"

"Did what, Charley?" asked Zell, looking up into her companion's face in surprise.

"Oh, I was just thinking how Dumars looked when you refused to dance with him. By thunder now, but it took the breath all out of him! I would hate to have you refuse me, if it would hurt me like it seemed to him. By jinks now, I will wait till I am right certain before I try it!" he muttered half aloud.

"If you were no more honorable than he is, I certainly would refuse you," she said, looking away, to hide her blushing cheeks.

"Ah," he muttered, "then I will try to be honorable, if that will help me to be successful."

"You couldn't be otherwise if you were to try," declared Zell frankly.

"Couldn't be otherwise than successful?" asked Charley quickly.

"Oh, I didn't say that," she replied with a peculiar emphasis upon the word say.

"Oh, but I hope you mean it, Zell," he pleaded.

"Oh, come, let's go home, Charley," murmured †
happy girl; for, somehow his word awakened a new a
happy hope in her heart.   But she was not quite p
pared for it yet, though she had seen, for some ti
past, that it was coming.   It was no surprise, yet it v
almost too much happiness, she thought, for such
unfortunate girl as she.

————:o:————

A SUICIDE.

CHAPTER XXXV.

LUCY'S DEATH.

The next day after the wedding, our four friends—Charley, Zell and the young married couple—started on their journey for Helena. Dumars and Lucy took the same stage with them.

"We have been intending to go for some time past," said Dumars, little suspecting that his plans were known by the detective and Zell.

The days were pleasant and the ride across the country to Gallatin was one of the most pleasant imaginable. The roads were good and the scenery grand and beautiful, and so quickly did the first few days pass by, that, almost before they were aware of it they had reached the town of Gallatin.

The morning of the day—Saturday—that they reached Gallatin, an old man, by the name of Dean, with his son, a lad of fourteen, and daughter, a very handsome, graceful girl of eighteen, took passage on the stage with them. They, too, were on their way to the new mines where an older son was living.

Here, they were to lay off over Sunday; and so they sought a hotel where they, and the old man and his children, remained. It had been a very quiet day, for Sunday in Gallatin was a dull day, and the time dragged slowly. But at last, evening came—a beautiful, moonlight evening; just such an evening as lovers are wont to choose for a ramble.

"Let's go down town, Zell, and see what we can find," said Charley, throwing down a novel which he had vainly been trying to interest himself in.

"I don't suppose you old folks want to go," said Zell, as she put on her hat and started off with her companion.

"Oh, no," laughed Kitty, "we will stay at home—we don't need any more moonlight rambles, so good-by, children."

"What shall we do, Zell, go to the opera or to church?" asked Charley, as they strolled down the street.

"Just as you please, Charley, I am not particular about either to-night," she answered.

"Neither am I, but here is an opera house; let's go a few minutes; I want to see if I can see anything of Dumars. I haven't seen him to-day, have you?"

"Why no, of course not; but I saw Lucy this afternoon," she replied.

The play was not interesting to either of them, and they were heartily glad when they got into the pleasant moonlight again.

"No," replied Charley; "they were not there."

"Did you see anything of Dumars?" asked Zell.

"I saw Lucy this afternoon; she is not well I think. I never saw her looking so badly as she did to-day," said Zell; "I don't think that Dumars treats her well."

"Do you believe that they are married, Zell?" queried Charley.

"Why I suppose so, of course—she says that they are."

"I don't believe it just the same!"

"Let's don't talk about that, Charley. Come, it isn't late, let's go down by the river," said Zell. "Oh, I wonder if we can't find a boat? I haven't had a boat ride since we came down from the mountains."

"We will see. We ought to be able to find one somewhere," said the detective, as they strolled along the sandy shore of the river. In a little while they had the satisfaction of finding a boat. Pushing the little boat into the stream, they seated themselves upon a seat together and each taking an oar, they rode out over the smooth, moonlit surface of the river.

"O how lovely! How beautiful! I could sail on like this all night and not tire," exclaimed Zell in a glad, happy tone.

"Beautiful indeed Zell, and with such a beautiful girl as you for a companion, I could almost wish to float on thus, down the bright, crystal tide of the beautiful river of life, always. For, indeed, beautiful and happy must be the life that shares a companionship with you, sweet, beautiful, little Zell, through life," murmured Charley, looking down into his companion's happy, blushing face, as she shyly met his keen, searching gaze. Volumes of love—the love of a pure and noble young heart, were expressed in her shy but unfaltering eyes.

The oars trailed listlessly in the rippling tide, while the little boat, as if it understood the situation, and left without a guiding hand, swung around and drifted aimlessly down the stream.

"Zell," whispered Charley, bending low over the blushing girl and pressing his lips to hers—to those sweet, ruby lips which had tempted him so often, yielding so readily, so lovingly, while her bosom heaved with that fierce, passionate love which was struggling within, "Zell, will you—"

O cruel fate! For at that very moment, that moment of all others when they should have been left alone, undisturbed; out upon the still night air, rang a low, frightened cry.

"O Charley!" cried Zell, starting up from her blissful dream, "what was that?"

Without a word Charley had seized the oars, and with long, swift and powerful strokes, sent the boat bounding away over the water in the direction from whence the sound came.

Standing in the bow of the boat, Zell watched, scanning the surface of the dark, cold water, closely, hoping, yet fearing, to see the object of their search.

On, on sped the little boat, over the silvery surface of the sluggish river, like a frightened bird. On swiftly now, when a cry from Zell, just as the boat struck something, brought Charley to his feet and to his companion's side.

A white object floated in the water beside the boat. In an instant Zell had grasped it and in another moment Charley's strong hand assisted her in raising the limp and apparently lifeless form of a fair young girl from the river.

"O my God!" cried Zell, as she gazed into the white, deathlike face, looking so pale and ghastly in the moonlight; "Charley, it is Lucy King."

"Poor girl!" said Charley pityingly. "Poor child; this is the sad sequel to a life of shame! Ah, had she a true and honorable friend in whom she could have trusted, this might not have happened."

"Sadly they bore the unfortunate girl to her hotel. A physician was summoned, but he declared that there was no hope.

All day Monday and Monday night they watched beside the dying girl, whose only wish, whose only prayer seemed to be, to see the man who had lured her to shame and to death.

"Oh Al," she moaned, "if I could only see you once more before I die, that I could forgive you, for I love you so!"   .

———:o:———

CHAPTER XXXVI.

FOILED.

"Who's this here, Mars or Dumars, that yer's a speakin' of, Jim?" querried Dick Taylor the outlaw chief, of whom we have heard mention before, as he and Jim Kingsbury stood in the road at the foot of a long and steep hill over which the stage road extended.

"Oh, he's a friend of mine, or rather of Kitty's. He is her husband, I suppose, for they were married, so they say, not long ago down at Hardscrabble," replied Jim.

"So they are comin' on with the covies, are they? Wall you've been workin' them pertty fine, I should say anyhow. So they arriv' at Gallatin Saturday, did they?" asked the outlaw.

"Yes; they stayed there yesterday and will be here to-night if nothing happens," replied Jim.

"Yes, 'cordin' to that they ought to be here to-night."

"They will be here all right. Tell every man to make sure of that detective; kill him on sight!" said Kingsbury nervously.

"Never yer fear; we'll settle his hash for him. If there's anything the boys 'd ruther do 's to eat, it's to kill a d—d detective. But why did you change yer first plans, do ye think this air's a better place for the job or what?" asked Taylor.

"No," replied Kingsbury, "not a better place, but a surer one."

THE MASSACRE.

"An' why'd yer think it air a surer one?"

"Well, the reason I think so is this: The night I wrote that letter, I had one of my cursed tantrums and, after finishing the letter, I went down to get a quieter and left the letter lying upon the table. I thought of it as soon as I got down there, and I hurried back as soon as I could, but still there was a plenty of time for any one that might have been watching to have went in and read a part of the letter at least. That cursed detective was there that night, so I learned afterward. I don't know that he was watching me, but there's no telling; so I thought it would be safer to change the place."

"Wall that was about right. I reckon it air the safest plan; but are you sure that they 'll be here to-night?"

"Yes," replied Kingsbury, "I met my friend, Dumars, at the Toll-gate last night and he told me that they arrived at Gallatin Saturday, and would start again Monday morning. John is driving, so we will have no trouble in stopping him. It was about eight o'clock this morning when I left him at the Toll-gate. He will stay there and Lucy will come on with her friends—Zell and Kitty."

"Who's this air Kitten anyway? Is she a girl?"

"Yes, she is a girl. She is married, but that don't hurt her, she's only a girl. She has been married only about a week, and is as sweet as a peach. You can have her if you want her."

"Bet yer life I want 'er," said the bandit chief.

"Well, come, it's time that we were arranging matters for their reception. It's nearly five o'clock; they will be here within half an hour," said Kingsbury; and together they turned from the road, and went back into the dense belt of heavy timber which skirted the margin of the swamp.

The men were soon called together and instructed even to the minutest details as to how they were to proceed. Every necessary arrangement was carefully made for the attack upon the stage upon which our friends were making their journey. The place chosen for the attack, was a dark, dreary swamp, the scene of many a heartless and bloody tragedy.

Situated as the swamp was, in a dark canon in the mountains, it offered every facility for an enemy to make an immediate and unsuspected attack upon passing stage or wagons; and it was here, that many such attacks had been made. Deep down in the dark shadows of this dismal swamp, the highway men were waiting in ambush, while Kingsbury and Taylor were posted in a position where they could see the road from the summit of the high ridge almost to the margin of the swamp. Here they were impatiently watching and waiting.

"Ah, look, look!" cried Jim in a subdued and excited tone. "Look, there they come." And he pointed to the top of the hill over which the stage was just coming.

The driver, after pausing for a few moments to allow his jaded horses to breathe, dashed on down the long, steep incline at a thundering pace toward the dark, gloomy swamp.

On thundered the coach. Now it had just reached the dreaded place, and the swamp, as if gloating in triumph over its unsuspecting victims, reached out its dark shadows like death's arms and seemed to draw the stage with its doomed victims into its cold, deadly embrace, into its very heart.

"Halt!"

The command rang out with terrible importance and with unmistakable distinctness upon the still evening air of that dismal swamp.

Oh, with what a chill of horror and dismay, did those ill fated travelers hear that brutal word of command. Cowering within the dark shadows of the coach, they awaited in fear and trembling.

At the word of command, a score of desperadoes sprang up around the stage, while the ominous click of as many guns sent a thrill of horror and dismay to the hearts of the five inmates of the besieged stage coach.

"Every man step right this here away, an' be mighty quick about it too, an' make no mistakes about it neither!" came in the heartless, cruel words of command from the bandit chief—Dick Taylor.

In a moment, the two men within the coach were dragged forth and, at the muzzles of a score of revolvers, were hurried off into the dark swamp.

As the men were hustled out of the coach, the bandit chief thrust his head through the door-way and peering within, he beheld the cowering, trembling forms of the three female occupants.

"Ha, ha," he laughed in his coarse, brutal voice, "ha, ha, my pretty bird! Right this way if yer please mum and be quick about it!" he said seizing the arm of one of the trembling, half fainting girls and, dragging her from the coach, he bore her away into the swamp.

"Great Jupiter," cried Kingsbury, as, after seeing the prisoners dragged away, he turned and entered the coach in the gloating, triumphant expectation of beholding his helpless victim—the beautiful Zell, "there's a mistake here! God," he cried, "who are you anyway? Speak!" he shouted, clutching the arm of a crouching female figure and half dragging her from the coach. "Treachery!" he fairly yelled, pushing the girl back into the stage and dashing away after the outlaws who had dragged the prisoners away.

"Hold, hold!" he shouted. "For God sake spare those men! There's a mistake here, there's treachery!"

But he was too late; for, already, the two men lay pale in death. Too faithfully had those heartless assassins obeyed the commands of their leader. The hardened, blood-stained outlaws had made no mistake, but had done their bloody work all but too well.

"What's ther row here anyhow?" demanded Taylor, approaching the excited Kingsbury.

"Row? row enough," fairly yelled the exasperated villain, as the horrible fact dawned upon his mind that, not only had a fearful mistake been made, but, what to him was still worse, he had been, in some unaccountable manner, completely foiled in his fiendish plot. "There's treachery here—"

"Curse you," shouted the excited and infuriated mob; "don't ye cuse us of treachery!" and, in an instant, knives and pistols gleamed in the fast gathering gloom.

"Hold on, boys, let's vestigate this air a leetle!" commanded the outlaw chief. "Splain matters Jems; what's ther row?"

"Explain nothing! No explanations are necessary! There's treach—there's a—a mistake here, somehow," he stammered. ''They are not the persons that we want at all !''

''The devil they ain't!'' exclaimed Taylor. ''Don't try ter run no gag on us, Jems; just fork over that thousand dollars if yer please an' makes no mistakes about it neither.''

''Not a single cent do I pay, till you fulfill the contract!'' cried Kingsbury in a rage.

''Better fork 'er over Jems,'' warned the outlaw; and there was a gleam of wicked triumph in his cruel eyes. ''You 'r 'sponsible for this air deed—my men made no mistakes here,'' pointing to the two murdered men, ''so anty up quicker 'n lighning!''

''Ho, here, you fellows!'' cried Kingsbury, as he handed the money to the robber captain. ''We have been betrayed, there's treachery somewhere, but I don't accuse any of you; it's Dumars! Ho! away then to the Toll-gate and bring him here! I left him there this morning; he's there yet!'' And in a few minutes, a half dozen horsemen were speeding away to bring the accused man.

''Curse the infernal luck!'' cried Jim, ''this will spoil my game—Hello! what in thunder is this?'' he demanded; he saw, for the first time, the fair and unconscious captive.

''Ha, ha,'' laughed the outlaw fiend, ''isn't she a beauty? This air is my prize!''

''Oh Taylor, this will never do; the whole country will be after us in no time!'' remonstrated Jim.

''Let 'em come!'' laughed Taylor. ''It 'll not be the first time they've been after us. I need this air bird for my nest!'' he declared.

"Ah! here they come with the traitor," cried Kingsbury excitedly, as the men returned with Dumars. "What, ho!" he shouted, "away with him! String him up!"

"For God sake, Jim," wailed the shivering, terrorstricken Dumars, "hear me; there's a mistake here; there's a—"

"Away with him!" yelled the infuriated Kingsbury. "String him up! String him up!"

"Hole don thar!" commanded Taylor. "Give ther feller a chance ter say his say!"

"Yes, yes," came from a dozen others, "let 'im say his say."

"So help me God," cried Dumars, "I know nothing of this matter!"

"But how in the name of tophet did it happen, then?" demanded Kingsbury. "There's something wrong somewhere."

"I don't know," replied Dumars. "Every thing was all right when I left."

"Didn't Lucy come on to the Tollgate?" asked Jim.

"No," replied Dumars.

"What do you suppose the reason is why she didn't come?"

"I can't even guess."

"You don't think that she has weakened and given our plans away, do you?"

"I don't know; she has been a little off for a day or two, but I never apprehended anything wrong," replied Dumars.

"No trouble between you and Lucy, is there?"

"No, no; she is subject to such spells ocasionally," said Dumars.

"But what are we to do, Dumars? The whole country will be up in arms against us in no time. Something must be done. In half an hour, Taylor will be off for his retreat in the canons of the Clay Mountains. There in the deep canons and almost inaccessible defiles they have their cabins."

"It's a duced shame," declared Dumars, "for that ugly villain to carry off that pretty girl!"

"Never mind the girl; we have all that we can possibly do to look after ourselves for a while at least, without thinking of her. The question now is, what are we to do?"

"Let's go back to Gallatin as soon as we can. No one will suspect us of complicity in this affair," said Dumars.

"Wall," querried Taylor approaching the two," 't won't do to dally any longer here; the jig's up for this hitch what conclusion have ye arin at?"

"We will have to lay for them again at some other time," said Jim. "We will go back to Gallatin and see what's the rip."

"All right!" said the outlaw, "I hope ye 'll come out all O. K.... If yer needs any more 'sistance, just drap us a keerd," he said; and turned back to his gang who were mounted and ready to go.

"Well, now then," said Kingsbury, "let's be off. Where are you and Lucy stopping?"

"At the Continental."

"And Zell and the others?"

"At the Windsor."

"Ah, well, I will go to La belle Kittie's.   Come on, let's be off."

"Perhaps, that we had better not go together," suggested Dumars.

"Perhaps not.   I will follow after, so you can ride on in advance."

"By thunder," muttered Dumars, as he rode rapidly away to Gallatin, "things are getting better every day! This thing must terminate before long; but how, that's the question?   The first thing for me to do, is to get rid of Lucy; but the question is, how am I to do it? · Once rid of her, there will be but two between me and Zell, and their taking off is already provided for.   This affair will necessarily make a change in our plans—Yes, I will do it!" he muttered, as some new thought seemed to strike him.   "Yes, I will send her on to Helena by the first stage and I will come on when I get ready—O yes! Ah, so then, I am virtually rid of you, Miss Lucy.   As for Jim, I will rid myself of him just as he thought to rid himself of me—just as he rid himself of John Barnes. But, first and worst of all, is that detective.   If Jim had succeeded here, as planned, all would have been well; but now, I am afraid, there will be a difficulty in getting him out of the way.   Once rid of him, I can do Jim up in a very short time."

"But what in the name of Satan has happened anyway?   Can it be possible that Lucy has betrayed us? No, no; that can't be; she is too faithful—she thinks too much of me," he said with a pang of regret for the injured girl.

Riding swiftly·on, he arrived at his destination a little

before daylight.　Delivering his horse to the stable boy, he repaired to Lucy's apartments at the hotel.

Somehow an uneasy feeling stole over him as he passed down the hall toward her room.　The door was partially open, and he could see that a dim light was burning within.

"Hello, here!" he exclaimed, in alarm, as he paused in the half open door of Lucy's room.　"What's up?"

By the dim light of the lamp burning low, he beheld a sight that sent a chill of horror to his guilty heart.

Lying upon the bed before him, dressed in her snow-white robe and with the palor of death upon her fair, young face, lay Lucy King, the girl who he had lured to dishonor, shame and death.　At her bed-side, sat Zell and the detective.

"Ah, Dumars," said the detective stepping quickly to the guilty man's side and, clutching his arm, "come here and behold the result of your villainous treachery!'

Slowly, the eyes of the dying girl opened and rested upon the face of her distroyer.

"Al!" she murmured faintly, "I am so glad that you have come back.　I wanted to see you once more before I die—Oh, we might have been so happy—but it s nearly over.　God forgive me, for I couldn t bear the thought of what would happen—the shame and disgrace of your unfaithfulness.　I forgive you, as I pray God to forgive me."

.　The white lips faltered; there was a gasp, a quiver of the lids as they closed over the blue eyes and the ashen palor of death took the place of the momentary flush that had suffused her pale cheek.　Lucy, wronged, broken-hearted Lucy was dead.

"Perhaps that you had better retire, Dumars," said the detective in a cold, stern tone. "Zell and I will watch till morning."

Without a word, Dumars turned and left the hotel.

Morning came ; and the funeral was over. The mourners—Dumars and our four young friends—turned from the grave after taking one last look and retraced their steps homeward.

"Dumars," said Charley, as they turned from the grave, "let me warn you: We know the story of this poor girl's shame. She has taken her life to escape a still greater disgrace. I could arrest you, and, if the people of this town knew the story of your damnable perfidy, you would never live to see the end of this day. Know, then, that it is by Lucy's earnest solicitation, her dying prayer, that you are allowed to go free. I warn you now—be very, very careful and not cross my path again!"

"Zell," said Charley, as Dumars hurried away, "I ought not to let that man go free!"

"But, Charley," said Zell pleadingly, "you know that I promised Lucy—"

"But Lucy will never know any differently," interrupted Charley.

"Charley!" cried Zell in tears.

"Well, it shall be on you, Zell," he said.

————·o:————

TO THE RESCUE.

CHAPTER XXXVII.

TO THE RESCUE.

"Ah, I wonder what is up now?" ejaculated Dumars, as he returned from the funeral and found a crowd of excited men gathered before the hotel." Perhaps I had better not go there. Ah, I will go down and see Jim and find out what's up. He feels a little sore about Lucy's death, but he suspects nothing," he mused, and he hurried down another street in order to avoid the crowd.

"Hello!" exclaimed Frank, as our four friends returned and saw the excited gathering which had given Dumars so much concern.

"I wonder what is the row here?"

"Go in with the girls, Frank, and I will see what's up," said the detective.

"It was Dick Taylor and his gang of cutthroats!" cried a score of voices.

Mingling with the crowd, the detective soon learned of the murderous attack upon the stage and the kidnapping of the unfortunate girl whose father and brother were killed in mistake for the detective and Frank, in the dark, dismal swamp.

"The wonder of it is," said one, "they didn't rob the stage."

"There must have been some other motive for the attack," declared another.

(225)

"Oh," exclaimed Charley, and he returned to the hotel parlor and related the story to his three companions and a few others that were gathered there; "I might have told them of the motive for that murderous attack—poor Lucy!" he murmured, "poor, wronged Lucy! In dying you have saved our lives though we could not save yours. "Zell," he said, "the fate of this poor girl has saved our lives. The story of her shame has led to the story of our lives. But this is not all," he said, and his voice assumed that deep, passionate tone which betrayed the pent-up passion of his noble heart. "This is not all, for they have, not only killed the old man and his son, but have carried that poor, little girl away."

"O God!" cried Zell; "Charley," she said, stepping before him, her voice trembling, her eyes flashing while her bosom heaved with that wild, uncontrollable passion, which, sometimes, was awakened within her brave, generous heart; "it was on our account that this outrage was committed—you must go to the rescue of this poor girl!"

"And I, too!" cried Frank.

"No, you will stay with the girls; I can get the help I need here," said the detective. And he left the room. Going down into the crowded barroom, he told of the plot to waylay and murder him and his friend Frank as the object of the attack upon the stage.

"Boys," he shouted, as he drew a revolver and waved it above his head," I am going to the rescue of that poor girl, to avenge the death of those two unfortunate travelers. Are there any here that will volunteer to help me? If there are, be here armed and mounted—I will start in five minutes."

Five minutes had passed and fifty armed and mounted men—the vigilants of Gallatin—stood before the hotel.

Down the steps, came the detective; then, pausing for a moment, before the rangers and the vast crowd, and raising his hand above his bared and bowed head, he said in a low, solemn tone—

"God willing, I will not rest till this outrage has been avenged!"

For a brief second he pressed the little hand that had stolen into his, and, with a quick, reassuring glance into those brave, hopeful eyes of his little companion, he sprang lightly into the saddle and dashed away with the bold rangers.

"To the dark canyons of the Clay Mountains!" shouted old Buckskin, the captain of the Rangers. And away they flew.

On, on, swiftly, they urged their panting steeds. All day and until late into the night which had closed around them dark and threatening. It was almost impossible to follow the trail by the dim, flickering light of their lanterns; but, fortunately, they had reached the mountains and had just entered a deep and narrow defile from which it would be impossible for the fugitive outlaws to escape.

"Out with the lights, boys," commanded the captain; "no need for them now." And again they urged their jaded horses forward.

For miles they followed the deep, winding defile. It was nearly morning and a slow, drizzling rain had set in; but still the dauntless rangers pressed onward. Suddenly, down the canyon, upon the beating wind and rain, was borne to the quick and practiced senses of the Ranger chief, the unmistakable scent of smouldering fire.

"Halt!" came in a low, cautious tone from the captain; and in a moment the men had dismounted and scouts were sent out to reconnoitre.

An hour passed and the scouts returned and reported that the outlaw camp was only about half a mile above, but was so strongly fortified by its natural surroundings that, unless they were to surprise them, an attack would be worse than useless.

"Everything is quiet," said an old scout," an' we kin surprise 'em."

"Take 'em a napping!" chimed in another.

"Forward then," commanded the old Ranger; and led the way.

Silently the dark figures, like shadows of death, stole upon the sleeping robbers' camp.

Now, they had reached the nearest house—a long, low, log-house. The men, drawn up in line, rushed forward and began the attack.

Wild and awful was the bloody scene, lit up by the flames of the burning cabins; many, whose inmates refused to come out, were shot down through the doors and loop-holes, or were roasted alive within.

The detective, with flaming torch, followed by a dozen brave, sturdy fellows, charged upon a house near the centre of the camp, and were met at the door by the outlaw chief himself. For a moment a fierce and bloody struggle waged; but they were soon overpowered.

Seeing his men shot down around him, the robber chief :urned and fled back into the house. Quick as thought, the detective divined his purpose, and darted forward and entered the cabin before Taylor could reach the room where his prisoner was confined.

"Curse you!" cried the detective, as he rushed upon the outlaw and struck him down with a blow from a heavy revolver. "Ah, but you didn't do it, my fine fellow. You thought to secure the girl and then, by threatening her life to compel us to some terms; but you are a little late."

"Hello here! here's the devil himself," cried a half dozen of the rangers as they entered.

"Whar's the gal, you bloody villain?" cried old Buckskin, applying the lighted end of his torch to the outlaw's nose.

"In there," sputtered the villain, pointing to the door. But the detective was there already; and, forcing the door open, he entered the room.

"Ah," exclaimed Charley, advancing toward the frightened girl. "Miss Dean, I believe. We are friends."

"O thank God!" exclaimed the girl. "O sir," she cried, "tell me, where is my father and brother!"

"Poor girl!" said the detective, as he looked away to shut out from his sight that look of despair. "Poor girl! your father and brother is dead."

"O God!" wailed the girl.

"Cheer up," said Charley, "you have friends."

"I have a brother at the new mines, where we were going," moaned the girl; "but I don't know how to get there."

"Don't worry yourself, my little friend, you will be provided for," answered Charley kindly.

"Whar's the kid?" queried old Buckskin, entering the room; "is she all right? "Ah," he exclaimed as he caught sight of her, "Little girl, you are all right, I guess."

"The work is done," declared another, and the men returned to the house, after having burned all the others. A few escaped, but not more than a half dozen.

"How many boys have we lost?" asked old Buckskin.

"Six," was the reply.

"Ah, well," he said," such is the lot of the Ranger."

Early in the morning, the dead Rangers were buried, and then the march homeward was begun. The progress was necessarily very slow on account of the wounded Rangers.

The next day, they were compelled to stop on account of the death of one of the boys. Here they stopped for a couple of days, waiting for teams which they had sent for to convey the wounded to the nearest settlement, where they could be cared for. Here also, a team was hired to convey the rescued girl back to Gallatin.

Again, as all were provided for as best it could be under the circumstances, they set out, in the morning of the fifth day since they started out on their errand of vengeance, on their homeward march.

Anxious to reach home, they concluded to stop for a few hours in the evening, and then again to resume the journey.

"We will get home about daylight I think," said the

detective, riding up beside the carriage in which the girl was riding.

"It is ten minutes past three now," she said.

"It's only about six miles farther," he said. "We will reach there in an hour and a half. We will be there in time for breakfast all right enough."

"Isn't that a carriage a coming over the hill there?" inquired the girl.

"Yes. Some one is out late. Some young fellows, I presume, returning from a trip to town," replied the detective, as he rode on to where a group of rangers were discussing the new arrivals.

———:o:———

CHAPTER XXXVIII.

KIDNAPPED.

"Now then," exclaimed Kingsbury, as he saw the Rangers ride away in pursuit of the outlaws, "we must act and at once."

"But how shall we act?" asked Dumars.

"We must devise some plan to kidnap Zell," replied Kingsbury. "You must lure her away somehow—"

"I can never do it, Jim," he replied. "Since Lucy's death, Zell—"

"Don't mention that again, curse you!" cried Kingsbury.

"Well, I can't do anything with her—ah, I have a plan," he said, as a new idea struck him. "Kitty loves dancing better than anything else on earth. Let's get up a grand masquerade ball, they will be sure to go. Nothing short of death could keep Kitty away from a ball. If she goes—and she will—Zell will go too."

"Good!" exclaimed Jim. "Go ahead with the arrangements and I will furnish the funds."

All arrangements were made and the grand ball announced. Three days had passed and the evening of the grand masquerade ball had rolled around. All Gallatin's fair belles and gallant beaus were in ecstacies over the prospect of the grandest turnout of the season.

" Oh Zell," exclaimed Kitty, "won't it be jolly?"

(232)

ZELL AT THE MASK BALL.

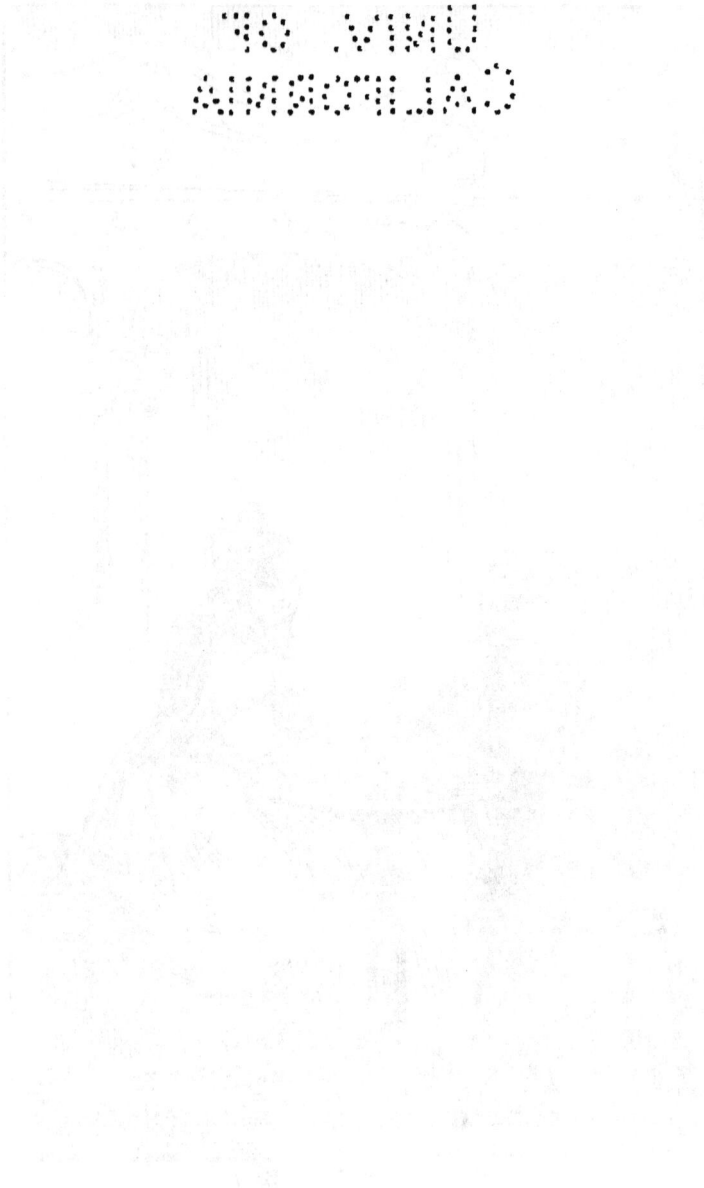

"Not for me. Kitty," answered Zell, doubtfully; "I don't want to go."

"Oh, but you will Zell, dear, won't you?" cried Kitty. "I have got everything arranged. I will go as a Scotch lassie, Frank will be a Paddy and you as a little Quakeress."

"But I don't believe that I—"

"Oh Zell," pleaded Kitty, "I am just dying to go. Do go Zell; please do, that's a darling!" .coaxed Kitty, throwing her arms around her cousin and nearly smothering her with kisses.

"Well, I suppose I will have to go, but I—"

"O goody, goody!" cried Kitty, spinning about the room in glee.

"O Kitty! won't you ever get over such foolish, wild fancies? You are a married woman now, and you ought to begin to quiet down a little," remonstrated Zell.

"Nonsense, Zell; just you wait until you and Charley are married, then you will know something about it!" laughed Kitty.

"I may have to remain a long time in ignorance, if I have to wait for that," replied Zell.

"Pooh! Fiddlesticks! Think you hat I have eyes, and can't see? Ears, and can't hear?"

"You see and hear more than I do, if you have seen or heard anything of that kind!" exclaimed Zell.

"O fie, Zell! Charley loves you desperately; you know he does. It's your own fault if he hasn't confessed yet."

"I don't know that it is; I am sure that I have not hindered him. I know that he loves me, but—"

"But nothing, Zell, dear! he loves you and you love him."

"Yes, I love him—"

"Heigho! talking of love, are you my dearies?" cried Frank, popping unexpectedly into the room. Guilty, guilty!" he laughed, seizing Zell's hand and looking down into her blushing face. "Ah, well, it's all right Zell! No one has a better right to love or be loved, nor is any one more or better loved than you are."

"Come, let me go!" cried the blushing girl, "It's time to dress for the ball;" and' freeing herself from her tormentors, she fled to her own room.

Down through the long hall, whirling and gliding, through the bewildering and intricate mazes of the Blue Danube Waltzes, merrily glided the belles and beaus of Gallatin. It was a joyous, happy throng. All—ah, no, not all; for there were two of that merry throng who were neither merry nor bent upon making merry. With this exception, all were bent upon having a merry time.

"Well, Dumars, what success now? Have you found out whether Zell is here or not?" asked Kingsbury, impatiently.

"Yes, she is here all right enough, but I haven't found her out yet. I have settled upon Frank and Kitty—"

"Hang Frank and Kitty!" interrupted Kingsbury. "It's Zell that we want to find."

"Ah, yes, of course; but in finding them we have gained much toward finding Zell. Watch them closely; the three will know each other, and will be together before very long," said Dumars.

"Where are they?" asked Kingsbury.

"See, just over there," and he pointed out the pair.

"Ah, the lass and the Paddy!"

"Yes. And do you see that little Quakeress? Keep your eye on her. I have seen her with them once; she is approaching them now. I believe that that little Quaker maid is Zell, said Dumars.

"Keep your eye on her," whispered Kingsbury, in a suppressed tone of excitement. "I will go and engage her for a dance. Under the influence of music, a little wine and a skillfully administered drug, it will be a very easy matter to lure her away," he said in a low tone. "So, watch and be ready. If you see us leave the room, follow immediately and help me get her to the carriage."

Approaching the sedate little Quakeress, Kingsbury, who was dressed to represent a dude, addressed the little Quakeress with—

"Ah, my dear friend, may I—ah, have the honor of your company for this—ah—exquisitely beautiful waltz?" he asked, as he courtesied in his most dudeish manner to the prim, little Quaker.

"Thank thee, lad," replied the shy little maid accepting his invitation; and away they went, mingling with the merry throng of dancers.

"Oh, how delightful," murmured Zell. "But I don't like him to hold me so close; but, then, they all do it. Oh, if it were only Charley, now, I would be so happy."

"Ah, my dear little lady," whispered the dude, "you are wearied. Come, a little refreshment will restore

you.   Waitah, a champaigne heah, if you please!" called
the dude as he led his companion to a little table.

"Ah, how delicious!" he exclaimed, holding the spark-
wine aloof, "let me fill your glass."

"No, thank thee; I do not drink wine," replied the
little Quakeress.

"Ah, but you will take a little," persisted the dude, as
he filled a glass.   "It will add lustre to those sparkling
eyes, it will—ah, paint roses on upon those hidden
cheeks.   Just a little, my sweet friend."

"Oh, thou flatterer!" exclaimed the little Quakeress,
just kissing the red wine with her still redder lips.

"Drink, drink!" eagerly urged the dude. "It will give
you new life, new joy, new and greater pleasure!" he
said.

"Oh," he thought, "if I could only compel her to
drink it!   Drink, drink," he urged again," just this one
little glass.

"Nay, nay," my friend; tempt me not so; it's a sin!'
she demurred.

"A sin! Ah, but I am acquainted with the gentleman.
Let me bring you a cream," he said, rising to go for it."

"Now," he mused, returning with the ice cream, "now
is my time; yes, I will flavor this to suit the occasion.
This flavoring is my especial favorite," he said; "try it
my deah lady."

"What a peculiar flavor!" she exclaimed, as she daint-
ily ate the cream.   "Indeed, this has a peculiar taste."

"Don't you like it?" he murmured; and there was a
gleam of triumph in his wicked eyes.

"No, I—I don't believe that I--do," she stammered;

for, already, the stupifying effects of the drug had begun to affect her.

"What a delightful evening!" exclaimed the dude, "let us go out upon the veranda for a moment and get a breath of fresh air. You feel uncomfortable; it is rather too close in here."

Dizzy and confused, she, almost unconscious of the act, allowed him to lead her out. Out upon the veranda, she felt the cool evening breeze upon her hot cheek and then, she knew no more.

Hardly had they reached the open air, when Dumars appeared and, together, they hurried the unconscious girl to the carriage which they had in waiting. Kingsbury entered the carriage with his victim, while Dumars mounted in front and drove swiftly away.

"Zell! Zell! Oh, where is Zell?" cried Kitty, rushing wildly into the dinning-room where the guests were already unmasking for supper.

In a few minutes, intense excitement prevailed. Search as they would, everywhere, no trace of the missing girl could be found. Wild with terror, Kitty rushed franticly about crying and sobbing hysterically.

There was no more dancing that night, and many left their supper untouched. But all effort to find a clue was without avail. No trace could be found.

"Another kidnapping within a week!" was the cry of the excited and infuriated citizens.

All the rest of that awful night, poor Kitty walked the floor of her room, moaning and sobbing in her grief, while out upon the streets crowds of armed and excited men gathered about and vainly striving to solve the mystery of the girl's disappearance.

It was nearly daylight, when a man came up to the crowd that had gathered in front of the hotel and reported that a carriage had been seen going out of town toward the west.

"After them!" cried a score of voices.

"Hold, here comes the Rangers!" cried some one; "Let's hear what they say."

————:O:————

A Lucky Shot.

CHAPTER XXXIX.

THE RANGERS' RETURN.

"By thunder, ejaculated old Buckskin, as the detective rode up, "them air fellers peer ter want to 'voide us, eh; suth'n' 's up, boys, let's 'vestigate!"

"Give chase," cried another, as the driver, after hesitating a moment, turned to the right and drove rapidly away, as if anxious to avoid the Rangers; "run 'em down!"

The detective and six others, putting spurs to their horses, dashed away in pursuit and were fast gaining upon the fleeing vehicle.

Not far ahead was a little stream skirted by a dense growth of willows and small trees, while just beyond was a heavy belt of timber. Just as the fugitive vehicle reached the brook, the driver was seen to spring from his post and disappear into the dark shades of the willows.

"Shoot 'em!" cried old Buckskin, discharging his revolver at the place where the man had disappeared. A dozen shots were fired, but so quick had been the man's flight, that he had made good his escape.

The fleeing horses, given their own head and frightened by the report of firearms, dashed away in their mad fury down a steep incline toward the river.

On, on, speed the frightened horses. Now the pursuers could see a man in the carriage vainly striving to reach the reins.

On, on. An hundred yards further, and they will reach the high bluff by the river over which they must, unless checked, be hurled upon the rocks below.

"Ah, steady there, steady!" cautioned old Buckskin, as he saw the detective rise slowly in his stirrups and bring his rifle to his shoulder. "Steady now, steady!"

One quick glance along the shining barrel and then, a puff of smoke, the red fire leapt from the deadly tube, and one of the horses crouching and quivering, staggered and fell almost upon the very brink of the bluff.

A crash, a scream, and, from the confused mass of carriage and horses, a man was seen to spring and quickly disappear over the bluff into the river.

As the carriage went down the scream of a woman was heard; and, in an instant the Rangers had gathered around and dragged the half unconscious form of a woman from its ruins.

"For God sake, Zell, what does this mean?" cried the detective, raising the frightened girl to her feet.

"O Charley, don't ask me now! I don't know how it happened. The last I can remember, I was at a ball. I ate ice cream with some one. I don't know what happened after that till I heard a terrible crash and then— but you know the rest," murmured Zell with a beseeching smile as she looked up into his honest gray eyes.

The boys, at the cross roads were watching the exciting race; and now, as they saw the victors returning, they sent up a shout that made the woods and hills resound with their glad shout of triumph.

"Miss Jessie Dean," said the detective as he returned, bringing the rescued girl to the carriage, "let me introduce you to my little friend Zell. "You will remember each other."

"Oh, I am so delighted to meet you again, Miss Zell." cried the girl joyously." "O Zell! your friend tells me that father and Willie were killed when the stage was attacked," and she burst into tears.

At sight of the poor girl's grief, Zell remembered her own father who had been so cruelly murdered in the dark forest. Thus, locked in each other's arms, they sat in the carriage as the now, doubly victorious rangers, again took up their homeward march.

A little before daybreak, the rangers reached the town, and, as they rode up, were greeted by wild shouts of triumph; for already the excited gathering could see the rescued girl. Wild and loud was the shout of greeting that went out from the throats of that motley crowd.

"O Charley!" cried Kitty, after the first excitement over the rescued one's return had subsided a little. "I want to confess: It was all my fault. I persuaded Zell to go to the masquerade. Forgive me, Charley; Oh, forgive me; I will never do it again!"

The story of the pursuit and the battle in the dark canyons was soon told, as well as Jessie's story of captivity.

"Then you will go with me, Jessie, and be my sister," declared the generous-hearted Zell.

"Oh, I would be so glad to go with you," said the unfortunate girl; "I will love you as only a sister can love."

"Thus it was arranged; and now, our company of friends increased to five, waited for the morrow to resume their journey.

CHAPTER XL.

The journey to the mines was accomplished. And eventful and pleasant, indeed, had been the trip; and many were the happy days spent by the young people. One, and only thing, can be mentioned as, in any way, tending to mar the pleasure and happiness of any one— that one was the brave, noble little Zell.

Jessie, after the first sharp pangs of grief for the loss of her father and brother had subsided, became her old self again,—a jolly, light-hearted, rollicking girl; who devoted herself with all the energy of a generous, loving heart to the entertainment of her new found friends.

Through Zell's heart, Jessie's warm affection and outspoken devotion to the detective for the inestimable service which he rendered her, sent a pang of jealousy. In vain did she try to convince herself that there was no cause for jealousy; but through all that long journey, the thought that the one whom she so dearly loved, to whom she had·given her whole heart, was loved by another.

Four months had passed and life at the mines had been both pleasant and profitable to all, or at least to all save two—Charley and Zell.

Gradually and unaccountably, an unnamable some-thing had sprung up between the lovers—a something

(242)

JESSIE.

that neither could see nor understand, nor how or why, neither could tell. But the demon, jealousy, had planted the seed and it had sprung up and grew till, at last, they came to look upon one another with distrust—or at least they thought that they distrusted one another.

"O Kitty," cried Zell, "I could die, I am so miserable!"

"Zell," said Kitty, "there's something wrong here. Charley loves you as dearly as any man can love. Why do you distrust him, Zell, why are you jealous of him?"

"I have no right to complain—I have no right to be jealous—Jessie has as much right to him as I, and I will not come between them! I love them both and will do all I can to make them happy!"

"But Zell, Charley doesn't love her as he loves you—"

"He loves me as a sister, that's all!" interrupted Zell. "If he wanted to marry me, he would tell me so," and she tried to look indifferent.

"Zell," said Kitty, "I think it is your fault, you are jealous and he knows it; but I don't think that Jessie knows anything about it. She is going with your brother Fred and I think that she is satisfied with him."

"O Kitty, don't lay all the blame to me! He loves me as a sister, no more," wailed the miserable girl. "Oh, I will go to him and I will tell him, and then, if I am wrong, I will beg his forgiveness!"

"Do, Zell, do, that's a good girl!" said Kitty. "Go to him, Zell, and confess just as we used to do. Go now, dear, while you have the courage. He is at home."

Zell turned and sought Charley who had just entered the home. He had been away for several weeks and had returned only the day before. He was sitting with his face buried in his hands, his elbows resting upon his knees and absorbed in thought. He was wondering over the strangeness that had sprung up between him and the girl that he loved so dearly and wondered how it all came about.

"Oh," he mused, "I will know, I will make her confess, I can't believe that she is jelaous of me, I know I liked Jessie and—ah, perhaps I didn't do just right, perhaps I ought to have confessed my love and asked her to marry me. I was going to ask her that night up on the river when we found poor Lucy. But I have no excuse for not telling her long before this."

"Charley," said Zell cutting short his meditations, "are you very busy, can you spare me a few minutes? I want to talk with you."

"Certainly, Zell; I can spare you all the time that you want, whether it be minutes or hours. But what is it, Zell?" he asked as he noticed her pale, troubled face.

"Not here, Charley," she said, "come with me."

"All right," he said and offering her his arm, they walked together down toward the little brook.

"Zell," said Charley, "I got a letter to-day from Helena. Kingsbury and Dumars have been there all the fall, I think, but they have left and I must go back there and see if I can trace them up again. I traced them there and located them about a week ago. They got wind of it somehow and have lit out again; and now I have this work to do all over again."

"Oh, I don't care," cried Zell, "let him go—"

"Zell," interrupted Charley, "what do you mean— what does all of this mean?" he asked as they paused

beneath the wide, spreading branches of the old oak tree
which served so many times before as a tristing place.
"Tell me, Zell," he demanded, in a low, passionate
tone, "tell me who has come between you and me!" I
have a right to know—I must, I will know!"

"Know, then," she cried, "it is Jessie Dean," and
with a haughty, defiant toss of her head, she turned and
walked away.

"O Zell!" came in a passionate, pleading tone.

Something in that pleading tone caused her to pause,
but only for a moment. A strange and almost un-
controlable desire to turn back came over her, but the
demon, jealousy, urged her on; and, with heart almost
bursting with grief, she walked on toward home.

"O that I had turned back!" she moaned. "I know
that he would have forgiven me. O God, forgive me
if I have wronged him!" Back to her own room she
hurried, and throwing herself upon her bed, she gave up
to her grief.

"Zell, Zell," cried Kitty entering her room, "what
have you done?"

"O Kitty, I don't know, I—I—"

"Quarrelled with Charley!" interrupted Kitty. "Oh,
how could you do it, Zell, how could you?"

"I don't know," moaned Zell, "I left him."

"No, no, Zell. O don't tell me it is so bad as that!"

"Go away, Kitty; leave me alone!" sobbed Zell. "It
is all over now, he will never forgive me—O that I
could die!"

"Leave them alone, Kitty," said Frank, when his
wife had told of the lovers. "It's only a lovers quarrel;
it will blow over in a little while; it will do them good."

But little did they dream what the result of that quarrel would be. Zell had determined to go away; and, when she had told Kitty of her determination, she added—

"I will go up to Ruby Gulch and visit Estella Lamorie. She has been wanting me to come and visit her ever since they moved up there. Don't object, Kitty; I think that I had better go away for a while, at least."

So it was arranged. Young Lamorie and his sister, Estella, came down after her, and soon, she was ready to go.

"I would like to see Charley before I go," said Zell. "I don't think that he would object, but I would like to have his consent."

"He has gone," said Kitty, "he went to Helena yesterday."

Jessie came over to see her friend off, little dreaming that she was the cause of her going.

"Oh, if I had only known," moaned Jessie, when, nearly two months after Zell had gone, she pursuaded Kitty to tell her why Zell had gone away, "if I had only known, this need not to have happened!" And burying her face in her hands she burst into tears. "To think she sobbed, "that I was the cause of all this trouble and I knew nothing about it. Oh, it is too bad!"

"Don't cry, Jessie," said Kitty, "you are not to blame."

"But I have been the cause of it, and I will never rest till I have made an effort to wright the wrong that has been done! Where is Charley?"

"He is at Helena," replied Kitty.

"Then I will write to him," said Jessie, rising to go home.

Returning home, she wrote a letter to the detective, and in concluding her letter she said—

"O Charley, you have wronged Zell, you have wronged me and you have wronged yourself in keeping this from me! If I had known, this would never have happened. Charley, if you love Zell, you will come home and go after her. Oh, if you only knew, what she must have suffered—for she loves you, Charley, as only a pure noble hearted girl can love, you would come home and go after her.

————:o:————

CHAPTER XLI.

DEEPER IN THE PLOT.

Ever since Zell had come to Ruby Gulch, she had been a prey to apprehension and fear. For, almost the first man whom she had met was Albert Dumars. Though she knew nothing of his connection with the kidnapping at Gallatin, she knew, from what the detective had told her, that he was in league with Kingsbury.

"Can it be possible," she asked herself, "that Kingsbury is following me?"

Nearly two months had passed, still nothing had happened to alarm her. Gradually, she had given up her seclusion and began to go out a little more.

One of her favorite pastimes was boating. Situated as the town was upon the shore of a beautiful little lake, she had the best facilities for enjoying this enchanting luxury. Along toward evening of nearly every fair day, she would take her little boat and row out into the lake, and nearly always alone.

This fact was seen and noted by two men who were stopping at Ruby Gulch. These two men—Dumars and Kingsbury—had noted, with a degree of triumphant satisfaction, impossible to describe, the fact that Zell nearly always went alone.

Kingsbury came to Ruby Gulch only occasionally and stayed but a few days at most at a time. He made his home at a place called the Fishers, situated on the opposite side of the lake.

(248)

"O! Let Me Die."

About this time, he had come over fully determined to
wait no longer, but to immediately carry out the plans
which he had arranged for kidnapping the girl. This
was nearly two months after Zell's arrival at Ruby.
There was only one thing that bothered him and that
was that neither he nor Jim could fathom the mystery or
object of Zell's coming to Ruby Gulch. Whether it was
some plan of the wily detective—a bait to lure them into
a trap, they could not even surmise.

"I don't like that mean business!" declared Dumars, as
Jim had declared his intention.

"But I have waited just as long as I can. Nearly two
months, and nothing done yet," said Jim.

"Ah, well, it will not be much longer that you will
have to wait; the plum is ripe, and this is my plan for
picking it: Nearly every evening, Zell is in the habit of
going out boating; she nearly always goes alone. Now,
get a boat—Jack and Fred will go with you—and watch
for her. I will get a boat and, disguised as the detective, will wait and watch too. Get in a convenient place
and wait till she is out far enough to make it safe, then
run her down and carry her off—"

"But why need we have two boats?" interrupted Jim.

"I am coming to that—I will wait, and when you
capture her, I will come to the rescue—do you catch on?
Overhauling you after we reach a safe point out of sight
of town, we will fight a sham battle; you will capture
me and hold me a prisoner. The girl will think that I
am the detective. She will marry you to save her life—
do you catch on?"

"Yes," replied Kingsbury, "and I will go over to the
Fishers and arrange everything, so that we can be mar-

ried within an hour after arriving there. It's a safe
place, and I can arrange it all right. There's but one
thing that might give us trouble, but we can arrange it
all right; and that is her answer, when asked by the
Justice if she will take me for her husband—"

"Ah, that is easy," interruped Dumars. "I will see
that no one hears her answer." So it was arranged; and
two days later Jim returned from the Fishers and
announced that all was ready.

"Now, Jim, a word for myself. I am out of funds—"

"All right," interrupted Jim, "here's a hundred dollars
—I will pay you the rest just as soon as the ceremony is
performed. Don't drink anything till we are through
with this job. I want your head to be clear."

"All right, I will wait."

Thus arranged, the two plotters awaited a favorable
opportunity, an opportunity which soon arrived.

Now, leaving them, we will return to the unfortunate
girl and see what she is doing. Ah, there she is, standing upon the front porch, watching the setting sun.

"Oh, what a lovely evening," she murmured. "The
setting sun paints such lovely, golden-tinted shadows
upon the lake. I believe I will run down just for a little
while to bid good-bye, for I will go home to-morrow."

Gliding quickly down to the shore, she stepped into
the little boat and was soon dancing merrily upon the
sparkling waters.

"Just one more ride," she murmured; "and then,
good-bye; for I go home to-morrow. Yes, I will return,
I will go back to him—to my lover, and ask his forgiveness—ask him to take me back to his heart again. Oh,

Charley, my darling, my darling!" and burying her face in her hands, she sat in silence thinking of things which are too sacred for other ears than the chosen ones to hear.

Presently, she was aroused from her reverie by the swift approach of a small sail-boat, which was heading directly toward her and was already within a few yards of her. Almost before she had time to realize what had happened, she found herself in the strange boat and speeding swiftly out into the lake.

Confused, bewildered and frightened, she sat in utter despair. Before her, gloating in his triumph, stood Kingsbury. But another object had now attracted the attention of the boatmen; and, with well feigned anxiety and fear, they watched the approaching boat, declaring that the solitary boatman was none other than the hated detective.

Oh, how wildly did the despairing heart of the poor captive throb within her bosom, as she recognized, as she supposed, the well known and dearly beloved friend.

On, on, sped the little boat; gaining rapidly now.

At last, with fearful oaths, the fugitives stopped and forced the coming conflict. The pursuing boat glided quickly along side, and then, commenced the sham battle in the fast gathering darkness.

Terror-stricken, the captive crouched in the bow of the boat and watched the conflict. It lasted but a few minutes, and then, the detective, as Zell supposed him to be, was overpowered and bound. One of the two men entered the captured boat and together the two boats continued across the lake.

As they sped onward toward the Fisher's, Kingsbury told the horrified girl of his intentions."

"Refuse me," said Kingsbury in a tone of villainous triumph, "and the detective shall die within an hour; marry me, and he shall go free. I have wealth; we will go to some foreign country where we can live in luxury. Everything that heart can desire, shall be yours. Do you accept? Shall your friend live? or will you refuse and let him die. Take your choice; but you shall be my wife whether or no. For so help me God, you shall be a wife this night!"

At last the Fishers—a small hamlet on the northern shore of the lake—was reached, and the captive *Zell* was taken to the place arranged for her reception, which was a low groggery kept by Dame Gostaff. "Here, Dame Gostaff," said Kingsbury, bringing his captive, "I have brought my betrothed wife; take her to her room and see that her wants are supplied."

"Yes, yes," cried Dame Gostaff gleefully. "I'll see that she wants nothing."

In the course of an hour, everything was ready and the guests were assembled in the barroom to witness the wedding.

"I will make a sure thing of it this time," said Kingsbury. "Ah, have a little wine for the girl; and here, put a drop of this in, just to quiet her nerves you know."

"Yes, yes," replied Dame Gostaff, "I understand."

Vile men and lewd women were gathered at Dame Gostaff's, in anticipation of a grand spree. They were all waiting for the appearance of the bride. At last, the door opened and she appeared leaning upon the arm of her intended."

"A little wine, Dame Gostaff," said Kingsbury, giving her a meaning look which she well understood.

"Yes, yes," replied the dame, and brought the wine.

"Stand up," commanded the Justice.

"Take this Zell," whispered Kingsbury; "it will make you feel better," and he handed her the wine.

"Stand up," said the official. "Do you take this air gal fer yer lawful wife, an' will yer love an' honor her an' pertec her, so long's yer live, so help ye God?"

"I will," replied Kingsbury.

"An' do you take this air man fur better an' fur wusser, an' will love an' honor an' oby 'im, so help ye God."

For a moment the poor girl was silent; but for a moment only. Then she answered—

"To save his life, O God! I will."

Not many who stood by heard her answer; for Dumars, who was standing by, drowned her answer by rushing forward and without waiting for the official to pronounce them man and wife, poured forth his congratulations, so as to drown her feeble words.

"Take her to her room, Dame Gostaff," and see that all is prepared for the coming of her lord and master!" commanded the triumphant villain. Then, turning to the crowd, said—

"Make merry, lads and lassies! Fill up the flowing bowl—fill it to the brim! for it's my treat to-night!"

It was midnight; the red wine and fiery liquor had flown freely; wild and lewd were the Bacchanalian orgies of that night. Loud, the siren songs rose above the music and the dance; when Kingsbury approached the vile hostess and said—

"Ah, Dame Gostaff, how fares the fair bride? Has she aroused yet from the effects of the drug?"

"Yes, yes," replied Dame Gostaff, "she is now ready for her lord."

"Ah, I will go to her then. Pass out the fiery liquor —pass it out freely, Dame Gostaff and I will pay on the morrow—good night."

Repairing to his wife's apartment he found her fully recovered from the stupifying effects of the drug.

"Ah," he murmured, advancing toward her; the villainous triumph gleaming from his snaky eyes; "Ah, Zell, at last you are my wife. Oh, I have waited long for this happy moment. Come, my darling bride— come—

But he did dot finish the sentence; for, uttering one wild, frightened scream, the horrified girl rushed from the room.

Down through the crowded bar-room and out into the night she rushed with the speed of a frightened deer.

"After her, after her!" shouted the baffled and exasperated villain. "Quick, quick! she's gone mad! Quick before she reaches the lake! She will drown herself! After her, quick! I will give a thousand dollars to the man that saves her!"

On, on flew the frightened, determined Zell. The shouts and hurrying footsteps of the pursuers only lent speed to her flight.

"O God!" she cried, "give me strength to reach the water. Let me die! O God! let me die!"

A moment more, and she had reached the shore where the water ran swift and deep, for a moment she paused, her white robe fluttered in the moonlight and then, a little frightened cry, a splash, a plunge and she was gone.

The dark, cold waters leapt above her frail form, and, like a demon's arms, seized upon the fair victim and bore her away.

"Too late, too late!" shouted the frustrated Kingsbury, as he saw her disappear beneath the dark, cruel waves. "Gone, gone!"

————:o:————

CHAPTER XLII.

It was midnight, and along the shore of the beautiful little lake that nestled so snugly among the snow bound mountains of the Cœur de Lion, could be seen, a little boat gliding silently and swiftly toward the Fishers.

"Ah, what is that, I wonder!" exclaimed the lone occupant of the little boat. "Great Jupiter!" he ejaculated, half rising in the boat and peering intently toward the Fishers. "God! it is a woman running toward the lake, and there are men following her, too!"

"On, on, little boat," urged the boatman; "speed now!" and turning its prow directly toward the point for which the fugitive was makking, it sped swiftly to the shore.

Out upon the still midnight air rang the shouts of the drunken mob. Then a white figure fluttered for a moment upon the rocky shore where the waves lashed themselves into foam upon the black rocks; then came a low, pitiful cry and the white robed figure disappeared, neath the dark, cold waves.

"God of Heaven!" cried the boatman, as the little boat dashed to the spot, and he saw the white garments, and the still, white, upturned face of the unfortunate girl.

Seizing her in his strong hands, he drew her quickly into the boat and hastily throwing his overcoat over her,

(256)

THE PURSUING BOAT.

he turned and confronted the mob who had gathered upon the shore.

"Ho, there!" cried Kingsbury. "bring her here. she is my wife, brin—"

But he never finished those words; for, quick as lightning the boatman's arm was raised; then came a bright flash, a sharp report followed by a horrible shriek, and Kingsbury, tottering for a moment upon the very spot where Zell had stood but a few moments before, pitched forward and disappeared beneath the seething waters below.

"Hounds of hell!" hissed the boatman, "back for your lives! I will shoot the first man that advances a step." So saying, he turned the boat into the lake and sped swiftly away in the direction of Ruby Gulch.

"To the boats," cried Dumars, "and after them!" And in a moment, the boat in which Dumars had come, was manned by himself, Jack and Fred—two of his old associates—and a few toughs of the place, and set out in pursuit.

Away over the angry waters of the lake, flew the pursued and pursuers. On, on, they flew. The wind had raised to almost a gale, and the little boat, bounding from billow to billow, dashed the cold spray into the pale face of the half unconscious girl as they flew onward.

"O God!" came in a feeble voice from the prostrate figure as she moved uneasily and attempted to 'rise. "Where am I?" she moaned. "O!" and a convulsive shudder passed over her as she remembered, with an awful, sickening feeling at her heart, the awful tragedy of that night.

She heard the splashing of water, and she knew that she was in a boat; and rising to a sitting posture, she saw the dark form of the boatman. He was gazing intently across the water. Following his gaze, she saw the pursuers. They were gaining rapidly now for the men, had taken the oars and were rowing to aid the sails in propelling the boat. They were scarcely a hundred yards distant now.

"Oh!" exclaimed Zell, with a shudder and covering her face with her hands, she endeavored to shut out the awful sight. For, at that moment, the boatman, bending slightly forward, raised a long, dark object which the girl knew was a rifle. For an instant he glanced along its shining barrel; then came a bright flash, a deafening report followed by a cry of pain from the pursuing boat.

Again, and again, came that deadly report, followed by that awful cry.

"Ah, I thought so," muttered the boatman, as the pursuing boat swung quickly to leeward and began speeding away. "Ha, ha," just one more!" said the avenger, "just a parting shot," and again he raised the rifle—

"Don't dont'!" pleaded Zell. "O Charley!" she cried, staggering forward and throwing her arms around the boatman's neck. "Don't! Oh don't do it again!" she pleaded, "let them go, Charley, let them go!"

"Zell!" he exclaimed, "Oh, I thank God that I was not too late! But tell me Zell, what has happened? How came you there, and why did you try to drown yourself?"

In a low tremulous tone, Zell told the story of that night of horror, of her abduction, of her forced marriage with Kingsbury.

"Oh," she cried, in a voice tremulous with emotion, ''I would a thousand times rather have died than to have let him—" here the poor girl completely broke down; and, hiding her face in his bosom, she burst into tears. But whether those tears were of grief or joy, let those who will, say.

"Charley," she asked, after choking down the sobs, "how did it happen? How came you there when I jumped into the lake?"

''I was looking for you, Zell," he replied, and in a few minutes he told her of Jessie's letter, and how he had come to Ruby Gulch after her. How, when he had reached the carriage he found that she was gone. No one knew where nor when she went.

''I met a little boy," he said, ''down by the lakeshore, and he told me that he saw you go out in a boat, and a little while after, he saw a boat with three men in it, run her down and carry her off. The boy said that the boat went directly across the lake. So," he said, ''I came here in hope of finding a trace of you.

For some time they stood in silence, then Zell, looking up into her lover's face asked in a low, beseeching tone—

"Charley, am I that man's wife?"

''No," he answered in a deep, passionate voice, ''no, you are no wife, little Zell Jim Kingsbury does not live!"

"O Charley!" cried the girl, her heart bounding with

hope, with love and joy at the glad news of her freedom and her enemy's death, "I owe all this to you—life, honor, everything! O that I had known what I now know, all this need not to have happened!"

"Zell," said the detective, taking her hands in his and looking down into her wide, blue eyes raised so beseechingly, so imploringly to his, "let the past be forgotten—forget and forgive."

"Can you forgive me, Charley? can you take me back to your heart again and love me as you loved me before? Can you trust me after all that I have done, after leaving you as I did that day down by the brook beneath the old oak tree? Oh, why did I do that, Charley? Why did you allow me to go?" cried the penitent girl through her sobs and tears.

"With all my heart, Zell, I can and do trust you. I love you now, Zell, better than I ever loved you before. Don't ask me to forgive you; it is I that should ask your forgiveness. I knew of your jealousy and it was not altogether without cause—and I ought to have done differently; but we don't always do just as we aught. We have both paid well for our folly and, I think, it will be a lesson that will last us the rest of our lives."

"O my generous, noble-hearted boy!" she murmured. "Oh, if you could only know how I have suffered you would say that I have been punished, and perhaps justly too, for my folly—"

"Don't Zell," pleaded Charley, "you are not alone in this; I too have suffered and was to blame. I ought to have known better than to allow such a thing to happen. I am older than you, and ought, at least, to have known better. But Zell, do you know that this has been the means whereby the work we undertook last spring has been accomplished—Jim Kingsbury is *dead*; our work is done."

"Thank God!" cried Zell.

"And my summer's vacation is ended."

"But you shall not go back!" declared the girl emphatically.

"It has been almost a year now since I got my vacation."

———:o:———

CHAPTER XLIII.

CONCLUSION.

Great was the rejoicing in the little home at Ceur De Lion when the truant was brought home.

The story of her exile, of her abduction, and her desperate attempt to escape by the sacrifice of her own life and the rescue, the flight and the deadly work of Charey's gun were soon told to wondering and awstricken friends.

"Now, then," said Frank Smith, "you have had all your say—I am going to have mine now! This thing has gone far enough, and I put the motion before the house that we have a wedding here to-night. The minister lives just across the street; in an hour it can be did."

"O! O! but won't that be jolly!" cried Kitty. "But want to amend that motion—here's brother Fred. and Jessie—here Miss Jessie, come back here; we are not through with you yet. Fred, go bring her back here—let's have a double wedding. It's so romantic and economical you know. Oh, you can't get away, little Jessie!" cried Kitty, as Fred returned with the blushing girl.

"Give us a week," pleaded Zell, "Jessie isn't quite ready yet."

So it was arranged. And, as the detective had some business at Ruby Gulch, he was instructed to invite Estella to the wedding.

Returning home on Saturday, Charley was met in the sitting room by Zell, carrying a little pink and white

(262)

THE DOUBLE WEDDING.

bundle in her arms, which she held out to him and, with a shy, roguish expression upon her happy face, said—

"See, Charley, what we have found; isn't she a beauty?" And they named her after me. Kiss her, Charley, you—no, no, you must not take her, you are too rough—kiss her, you are too rough—kiss her. There —O! you kissed her right on the nose! Arn't she nice?"

"Oh yes, it is awful nice, I guess," he said doubtfully, as the little lady resented the awkward kiss by yelling lustily.

"Zell, Zell," cried Kitty from her room. "What are you doing with my baby?"

"Oh, Charley kissed her," laughed Zell, carrying the little cherub back to its happy mother.

"I suppose I ought to congratulate you," said Charley, coming to the bedside, and, stooping down, he kissed the happy, young mother, "but I don't know just how to do it. Anyhow, she's nice and you did splendidly, so there!"

"Thank you, Charley; perhaps I may have an opportunity to return the compliment by and by," said Kitty.

Just then some neighbors came to see the new baby— the first born at Ceur De Lion.

The wedding day arrived and it was to be a grand event, for it was the first wedding at the mines. All Ceur De Lion was togged out in their "Sunday clothes." In a large tent, that served as a church, the ceremony was performed and the happy couples were united.

As they wended their way homeward, a miserable figure with bloated, besotted face—the very picture of a wretched, drunken bloat, tottering upon the verge of a drunkard's grave, who, for a moment, had paused before the church door, was heard to mutter, as he turned and staggered away—

·'Happy Zell!" and Dumars turned away from the happy scene and returned again to the dark dens of sin and shame.

What more is there to tell?

Nothing.

Thus, briefly told, ends the story of a ''Summer s Vacation."

''Ah, but it has not ended yet," says the detective, ''for I have not gone back."

And, as he said it, he saw the realization of that happy dream which he had seen in a vision those awful few days that he and Zell passed in the dark, gloomy cave—two bright-eyed, laughing children clambering upon his knees, pulling at his ears and whiskers or twining their tiny arms about his neck, while a slight, girlish figure flitted about, the fairy queen of his heart and home.

THE END.

—:o:——

www.ingramcontent.com/pod-product-compliance
Lightning Source LLC
Chambersburg PA
CBHW021113270326
41929CB00009B/867